Advanced Listening and Speaking

CAE

Kathy Gude

NEW EDITION

Oxford University Press, Great Clarendon Street, Oxford OX2 6DP

Oxford   New York
Athens   Auckland   Bangkok   Bogotá
Buenos Aires   Calcutta   Cape Town   Chennai
Dar es Salaam   Delhi   Florence   Hong Kong
Istanbul   Karachi   Kuala Lumpur   Madrid
Melbourne   Mexico City   Mumbai   Nairobi
Paris   São Paulo   Singapore   Taipei   Tokyo
Toronto   Warsaw

and associated companies in
Berlin   Ibadan

OXFORD and OXFORD ENGLISH
are trade marks of Oxford University Press

ISBN 0 19 453425 1
© Oxford University Press 1999

No unauthorized photocopying

All rights reserved. No part of this publication may be reproduced, stored in a retrieval system, or transmitted, in any form or by any means, electronic, mechanical, photocopying, recording or otherwise, without the prior written permission of Oxford University Press.

This book is sold subject to the condition that it shall not, by way of trade or otherwise, be lent, resold, hired out, or otherwise circulated without the publisher's prior consent in any form of binding or cover other than that in which it is published and without a similar condition including this condition being imposed on the subsequent purchaser.

Origination by Blenheim Colour Ltd, Eynsham, Oxford

Printed in Hong Kong

Acknowledgements

The Publisher and author would like to thank the following for permission to reproduce photographs:

Andes Press Agency/Carlos Reyes Manzo; Ardea/Jean Paul Ferrero, Jean Michel Labat, Joanna Van Gruisen, Tom Willock; Apple Macintosh; Artaud Freres - Editeurs; GIR34422 Dr Paul Gachet by Vincent Van Gogh (1853–90) Musée d'Orsay, Paris/Giraudon/Bridgeman Art Library, London; British Telecom; São Paolo, 1960, by René Burri/Magnum; Canary Wharf Management; Columbia/Irving Allen (Courtesy The Kobal Collection); Eye Ubiquitous/Tony Brown,Gary Trotter; Howard Fried-Booth; Friends of Save-A-Can; The Guardian; Sally and Richard Greenhill; Lionel Hampton; Louis Hellman; Kobal Collection/Columbia; John Cleare Mountain Camera; Mary Evans Picture Library; Nintendo; Popperfoto; Graham Rawle from Graham Rawle's Wonder Book of Fun, paperback £6.99/Victor Gollancz; Rex/Sipa Press; Ross Parry Agency; Royal Doulton; Royal Society of British Sculptors/Stephen Duncan, Georgina Redfern, Paul Riley, Alan Waters; Sun Alliance; Swift/Richard White Advertising; Time Magazine; Top Flight Loft Conversions, Edward Woodman.

Illustrations by:

Anna Brookes p. 88, 1.5, Nicki Elson p. 58, Neil Gower p. 17, 29, 47, 56, 57, 62, 93, 95, Sharon Palent/Maggie Mundy Agency p. 13, 112, Geo Parkin p. 19, 22, 27, 59, Tim Slade p. 61, 110, Harry Venning p. 23, 24, 24, 30.

The Publisher and author would also like to thank all those who participated in the research and development of the book, in particular the following for their valuable advice:
Caroline Coate, Sara Evans/Cultura Inglesa Copacabana, Angela ffrench, Diane Fleming, Rosalie Kerr, Ann Whitfield, Jennifer Whyte, Simon Williams.

THE EXAM

LISTENING: CAE PAPER 4

Format
The Listening Test consists of 4 listening texts: Parts 1, 2, 3 and 4. These texts differ in length and test listening skills through a variety of question types e.g. note-taking, sentence completion, multiple matching, identifying statements speakers made, and multiple choice questions.

Timing
The Listening Test takes about 45 minutes and contains between 30 and 40 questions. You hear Parts 1, 3 and 4 twice, whereas you hear Part 2 only once.

What you have to do
You have time to read through each task before you listen to the recorded text. As you listen, you must write your answers on a question paper then transfer them to an answer sheet. You will have ten minutes for this transferral at the end of the test.

What is being tested
The Listening Test requires you to listen for both global and specific information. Parts 1 and 2 test your understanding and application of specific information from the text. Part 3 tests your understanding of gist, attitude and directly stated information. Part 4 tests your understanding of context, opinion, speaker identity, etc.

A note on spelling
When writing answers, you are expected to spell correctly, but you are not penalized for the wrong spelling of a proper noun if you write an acceptable alternative.

How this book will help you
The book gives you practice in listening to each other in class, to the teacher and to the cassette recordings. These recordings differ in length, i.e. from short snippets of conversation to longer talks and conversations, and the speakers have a range of accents, all of which will help to build your confidence in interpreting what you hear in the exam itself. The book gives you useful advice and practice for writing notes and processing information while you listen, and it helps you to decide what to listen for, and to interpret meaning dependent on intonation, stress patterns, rhythm, juncture and phonology. There are also many different task types which prepare you for what you might find in the exam.

SPEAKING: CAE PAPER 5

Format
The Speaking Test is conducted by two examiners, one of whom acts as Assessor, the other as Interlocutor (the speaking examiner). You are examined in pairs, or occasionally in a group of three, should there be an odd number of candidates in an examining session. There are 4 Parts in the Speaking Test. In each of these Parts, you respond to visual or spoken prompts which are designed to elicit different speaking skills.

Timing
The Test takes 15 minutes for a pair of candidates.

What you have to do
In Part 1, you are given an opportunity to interact socially. Part 2 gives each of you an individual turn of one minute (this is known as a long transactional turn). In Part 3, you take part in a problem-solving task together. In Part 4, the discussion related to Part 3 is widened and the examiner joins in.

What is being tested
Throughout the test you are being assessed on your Grammar and Vocabulary, Discourse Management, Pronunciation and Interactive Communication. You are given a mark for each category, plus a mark for Global Achievement by the Interlocutor.

A note on Discourse Management
This is your ability to combine your language and ideas to produce connected speech. It refers to 'internal coherence', which conveys your ability to organize your sentences using, e.g. link words, pronouns, reference devices, to express yourself effectively and communicate your message.

A note on task achievement
The attempt to complete the tasks is assessed, not arriving at a 'right' answer within the time available.

A note on pronunciation
Examiners do not expect you to have a 'perfect' English accent! However, they do expect you to speak clearly and unambiguously so that what you say is easily understood.

How this book will help you
The book covers, in a systematic and comprehensive way, the skills you need to listen and speak, and also to process and exchange information while you are doing so. By analysing the Function Files you can develop an awareness of what an appropriate comment would be, and then use it in context. This book helps you to handle pronunciation features (i.e. stress, rhythm, juncture and phonology) effectively, thus preventing any breakdown in communication. Furthermore, successful task completion in the exam depends on your being able to produce the right kind of language in an appropriate way. The book helps you to do this by focusing on register, social interaction, structure and vocabulary at each successive stage of the Speaking Test.

Contents

THE BOOK

Aims
The Modules are designed to help you acquire and practise in a systematic and comprehensive way the skills you need to do your best in both the Speaking and the Listening Tests.

Contents
Advanced Listening and Speaking (CAE) consists of 21 self-contained Modules which you can use either as a supplement to a course book or as part of a skills course. The 'stand-alone' Modules can be used in any order, depending on your individual needs and interests, apart from Module 1A *Getting to know you*, which is intended to be used at the beginning of a course. Each Module is designed to take about 30 to 40 minutes, depending on the number of students in your class, and the number of activities you do.

Organization
There are six sets of Modules. For easy reference, the odd-numbered groups have particular (but not exclusive) focus on Paper 5, while the even-numbered sets focus on Paper 4. Each Module deals with one Part of these Papers. For example, Modules 1C/D and 3C/D concentrate on Paper 5, Parts 3 and 4; Modules 2B and 4B concentrate on Paper 4 Part 2.

Exam practice
At the end of each Module in the first four sets, there is an exam-type exercise. The last two sets provide a bank of tasks for Papers 5 and 4 respectively, recycling the material in the first four sets. You can use the tasks in the bank either to supplement the activities in the earlier Modules, or for exam practice.

Special features
The first four sets of Modules (1A to 4D) are interspersed with exam hints and Function File Cards containing expressions and phrases for you to analyse, then use while you are taking part in the speaking activities.

The book at a glance
Spotlight on Paper 5 *Speaking*
Modules 1A, 1B, 1C/D
Modules 3A, 3B, 3C/D
Task Bank Modules 5A, 5B, 5C/D

Spotlight on Paper 4 *Listening*
Modules 2A, 2B, 2C, 2D
Modules 4A, 4B, 4C, 4D
Task Bank Modules 6A, 6B, 6C, 6D

FUNCTION FILE INDEX

Admitting that you might be mistaken	20
Advising someone (not) to do something	32
Agreement	
Asking if someone agrees	54
Finding out if everyone agrees	21
Arguing against	63
Arguing for	62
Asking someone to repeat something	52
Certainty, possibility and improbability	43
Choosing	60
Commenting on something you know nothing about	21
Comparing	55
Correcting what is not accurate	35
Describing location	13
Describing similarities and differences	13
Disagreeing politely	19
Feelings	
Explaining how you feel about something	56
Giving yourself time to think	49
Interpreting past ideas	44
Linking contrasting ideas	49
Opinions	
Asking for the opinion of others	16
Giving your opinion	16
Putting forward another point of view	33
People	
Finding out about people	8
Finding out if people know each other	6
Introductions	7
Preferences	17
Saying something is (in)appropriate	59
Saying something is or isn't fashionable	60
Saying you are interested	58
Saying you aren't interested	59
Saying you aren't sure	75
Saying you'd like to	75
Saying you'd rather not	75
Speculating	10
Speculating about what you hear	23
Spelling	25
Summing up	58
Wishes and regrets	47

1 SPEAKING

Module 1A Getting to know you — 6
Meeting and finding out about people, introductions, personal questions, vowel sounds, recognizing names.

Module 1B People and places — 10
Speculating, describing, word stress, comparing and contrasting.

Module 1C/D Jobs and training — 16
Exchanging opinions, expressing preferences, personal information, sound discrimination, reaching an agreement, developing the interaction.

2 LISTENING

Module 2A Sorry, I didn't quite catch that! — 23
Coping with accents and background noise, making informed guesses, recognizing words, evaluating differences, spelling.

Module 2B Leisure activities and holidays — 29
Making assumptions, word stress, interpreting and rephrasing information, giving advice, identifying recycled information, putting forward another point of view.

Module 2C Mind over matter — 34
Interpreting unusual information, making notes while listening, listening for key information.

Module 2D Today's technology — 38
Interpreting visual information, interpreting attitudes, identifying speakers, sound discrimination, matching information to speakers, anticipating what you are going to hear.

3 SPEAKING

Module 3A What if...? — 43
Past and future: degrees of certainty, predicting, hypothesizing, word stress, expressing wishes and regrets.

Module 3B Yesterday and today — 48
Comparing and contrasting, describing differences in attitude, variable word stress, asking for clarification, asking if someone agrees.

Module 3C/D Art and culture — 58
Expressing interest and taste, making a choice, arguing for and against, collaborating.

4 LISTENING

Module 4A Achievements — 66
Listening for precise information, interpreting in depth, predicting, recognizing words in context, following a line of development.

Module 4B Survival — 71
Relating what you see to what you hear, evaluating arguments, identifying recycled information, spelling, variable word stress, saying how you feel.

Module 4C A question of gender — 76
Evaluating preconceptions, listening for facts and figures, interpreting information, using notes, matching sounds to spellings.

Module 4D Points of view — 81
Understanding different points of view, homophones, identifying speakers, identifying points speakers are making, spelling.

5 PAPER 5 TASK BANK

Task bank 5A — 86
Six activities for Paper 5, Part 1

Task bank 5B — 88
Twelve activities for Paper 5, Part 2

Task bank 5C/D — 91
Six activities for Paper 5, Parts 3 and 4

6 PAPER 4 TASK BANK

Task bank 6A — 96
Four activities for Paper 4, Part 1

Task bank 6B — 98
Four activities for Paper 4, Part 2

Task bank 6C — 100
Four activities for Paper 4, Part 3

Task bank 6D — 104
Four activities for Paper 4, Part 4

1 SPEAKING

A Getting to know you

B People and places

C/D Jobs and training

1A Getting to know you

Spotlight on Paper 5 Part 1

1.0 🎤 **Finding out if people know each other**

In groups of three or four take it in turns to find out if the other students knew each other before starting this course. If they did, find out how long they have known each other and where they first met. Before you start, refer to the Function File card.

FINDING OUT IF PEOPLE KNOW EACH OTHER

Which expressions sound too formal for this situation?
Which expressions do you feel are the most appropriate?

Questions
Have you met before?
Do you know each other?
Have you two been introduced?
*Did you know each other
before you (came to the class)?*
*Had you met each other
before you (started the course)?*
*How long have you known
each other?*

Replies
*We met each other for the first
time today.*
*We've known each other for
(two years), since (we were at
school).*
We first met when we . . .
We haven't been introduced.

Getting to know you • Module 1A

2.0 🎧 Introducing yourself to others
Informal and formal language

Listen to three short conversations once and indicate their level of formality by choosing a number from 1 to 5, where 1 is very informal and 5 very formal.

Conversation A _____

Conversation B _____

Conversation C _____

Compare your answers with a partner. Did you agree?
What made you decide on the level of formality? Who might the people in the conversations be?

2.1 🎤 Deciding on levels of formality
Groupwork

Remembering what you heard in 2.0, what would be appropriate introductions in these situations?

1. speaking on the telephone to a service engineer who will call on you tomorrow to repair your washing machine
2. enquiring about your flight tickets to New York, which have not arrived
3. being interviewed for a job by someone you have already met briefly
4. talking to guests at a formal dinner party
5. meeting a friend's new boyfriend / girlfriend
6. introducing yourself to a new neighbour

Compare your decisions with those of another group.

2.2 🎤 Introducing other people
Levels of formality

INTRODUCING OTHER PEOPLE AND RESPONDING APPROPRIATELY

Match the introductions with suitable responses.
Which word is rarely used in spoken English but often in written English?
Why is it used?
Which expression sounds rather formal?

Introductions
I'm Maria and this is Louis.
I'm Maria Monteno and this is my colleague Louis Ferrand.
Good morning / afternoon / evening. I'm Dr, Mr, Mrs, Miss, Ms, ___ and I would like to introduce you to my colleague Dr, Mr, Mrs, Miss, Ms, ___

Responses
How do you do?
Hello.
Delighted to make your acquaintance.
Hi there! Good to see you!
Pleased to meet you!

Can you add any other introductions and responses to the lists?

Module 1A • Speaking

Exam hint

The examiner will ask you to identify yourself usually by saying either 'You are . . .?' and waiting for you to supply the answer, or by asking 'Are you Maria / Louis ?' It is enough to say either *Maria Monteno / Louis Ferrand* in the first case, or to answer *Yes, (that's right)* in the second.

Write your full name and title, e.g. *Miss* or *Ms Maria Monteno, Mr Louis Ferrand*, on a piece of paper and place it on the desk in front of you so that the other students can see it.

In small groups take it in turns to introduce each other in the following roles. Use appropriate expressions from the Function File card.

a   potential clients to a bank manager
b   your friends to your brother / sister
c   your family to your child's teacher
d   yourselves as candidates to an examiner
e   some business colleagues to your family

3.0 🎧 Talking about yourself

Making notes

Listen once to a man introducing himself to a group of people. As you listen try to remember and note down as many details as possible about what he says, then compare your notes with a partner's.

Was the task challenging? Why?

3.1 🎤 Finding out about your partner

Exam hint

Listening carefully and attentively to what is being said will help you to remember what you hear. Try this tip for concentration training: erase from your mind anything which could distract you, e.g. background noises, room temperature, personal problems, exam nerves, and focus your mind exclusively on the task you have to do.

> **FINDING OUT ABOUT PEOPLE**
>
> Which question might be considered an invasion of privacy?
> Would any of these questions be considered an invasion of privacy in your country?
> What kinds of questions *would* be considered an invasion of privacy in your country?
> Add more questions of your own to the list.
>
> *Where do you come from? Are you married / engaged / single?*
> *What are your interests / hobbies?*
> *What do you enjoy doing in your spare time?*
> *Why are you studying English?*
> *Do you have any special reason for studying English?*
> *What do you study / do for a living?*
> *How much money do you earn?*
> *What do you hope to do in the future?*

Interactive skills

Give the teacher the piece of paper with your name on it (written for 2.2 above). The teacher will pick out pairs of names at random. You have three or four minutes to find out as much as possible about your new partner.
You could ask about their:

- background.
- interests.
- reasons for studying English.
- career / studies.
- plans for the future.

3.2 🎤 Preparing a reference file of personal questions

Exam hint
Being able to ask questions will help you in Part 1 of Paper 5.

In groups of three or four, produce a reference file of personal questions which you could use to find out some information about your fellow students. Your teacher will check your file for appropriacy and accuracy.

Personal questions

How long have you lived here?
Where do you work?

4.0 🎤 Improving your pronunciation

A With a partner, read out the words below and comment on the differences in pronunciation and what might cause those differences. Don't worry if you don't recognize the words – some of them don't exist! Just try and guess their pronunciation.

1 bat   bet   bit   bot   but
2 bate   bete   bite   bote   bute
3 batter better bitter botter butter
4 bater beter biter boter buter

Take it in turns to read out one of the words in each line and see if your partner can recognize it.

B Read out one word from the pairs in columns 1 and 2 below and see if your partner can identify which word you are saying.

1	2
ship	sheep
blip	bleep
hip	heap
knit	neat
pitch	peach
rich	reach
ill	eel
mill	meal
is	ease
live	leave

4.1 🎧 Recognizing the names of people and places

Sound discrimination

Listen to six 'mini-conversations' and circle the names you hear on the tape.

1 Hurt   Hart
2 Wilt   Welt
3 Manton   Menton
4 Grasslands Gracelands
5 Lowland   Roland
6 Pond   Bond

What about your own name? Do people have problems spelling it?
Spell your own first name for the person sitting next to you then see if you can spell their first name and family name.

Module 1B • Speaking

> **Exam hint**
> Remember, the second examiner, the Assessor, does not take part in the Speaking Test and is only introduced briefly to the candidates in Part 1.

🎤 Exam practice: social interaction

Divide into groups of four or five. (If there is an odd number of candidates for the speaking test it is necessary to have one group of three candidates.) Take the following roles. Allow three or four minutes for the interaction.

Two (or three) students: candidates A and B (and C)
One student: the 'talking' examiner (Interlocutor)
One student: the 'listening' examiner (Assessor)

Interlocutor:	Welcome the candidates and introduce yourself and your colleague.
Candidates:	Respond appropriately.
Interlocutor:	Check the identity of the candidates.
Candidates:	Respond appropriately.
Interlocutor:	Ask candidates either to tell you about or to find out about the other candidates.
Candidates:	Respond as appropriate.
Assessor:	Check the timing.

Now reverse roles with the two examiners taking on the roles of candidates.

There are more Paper 5 Part 1 tasks in the Task bank on pages 86–88.

1B People and places

Spotlight on Paper 5 Part 2

1.0

🎤 Speculating

> **SPECULATING**
>
> Which expression sounds too formal for an exam situation?
> Which sounds too off-hand and too informal?
> What is the meaning of *might, could* and *must* in these expressions?
> Add expressions of your own to the list.
>
> ... *might / could / could well (be) / must (be)*
> *Who knows?*
> *They / He / She look(s) like ...*
> *They look as if (they are) ...*
> *One can't rule out the possibility that ...*

> **Exam hint**
> Even if you haven't got a clue, don't keep silent. Have a verbal, not a mental, guess! You are not being examined on your ideas – just your ability to express them in English.

The nine pictures opposite show three men as babies, teenagers and adults, but the pictures have been mixed up. In pairs or groups, decide which pictures might be of the same person.

People and places • Module 1B

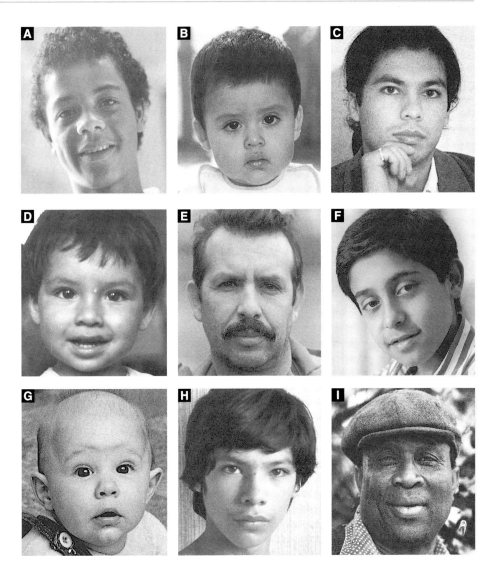

Optional activity

Bring in photographs of yourselves as babies or young children, place them all together on a desk and see if you can guess which photograph belongs to whom!

1.1 🎤 **Describing people**

Combine the words on the left with those on the right to make useful phrases for describing people. How many of them can you use to describe the people in the pictures?

1	bushy	a	moustache
2	straight	b	cheeks
3	curly	c	eyes
4	oval / round	d	build
5	rosy	e	nose
6	slim	f	face
7	turned-up	g	hair
8	handlebar	h	eyebrows
9	well	i	height
10	of medium	j	built

Module 1B • Speaking

1.2

Exam hint

In Part 2 of Paper 5, you will be asked to talk about something for one minute. Practising will help you realize how much talking you are able to do in this time.

🎤 Talking for one minute

Choose one set of pictures in 1.0 which you think are of the same person and describe them to a partner, explaining how the person has changed physically over the years.

Say what kind of job you think the person might have now and what he might be like, e.g. easy-going, bad-tempered, organized, friendly. You can use your imagination and speculate. The Function File card in 1.0 will help you. You have about one minute for this. Your teacher will tell you all when to start and finish.

After you have finished see if your partner agrees with your opinion, then listen to your partner describing another person.

2.0

🎧 Extracting information and drawing

Find the suspect

You will hear part of a radio news item about an armed robbery. As you listen to a description of someone wanted in connection with the crime, try to sketch *an impression* of the person in the empty box below.

WANTED
in connection with an armed robbery

Compare your drawing with a partner's and decide together what the character of this person may be like and why the person might have become involved in this robbery in the first place.

People and places • Module 1B

2.1 🎤 Describing location and spotting similarities and differences

Bank interiors (Pairwork)

DESCRIBING LOCATION

Which information would the examiner not be particularly interested in hearing? Why not?

at the very top / bottom of the picture
in the top / bottom right- / left-hand corner
on the left- / right-hand side
in the foreground / background
two centimetres from the left- / right-hand side
right next to
just / a little to the right / left of
directly opposite

DESCRIBING SIMILARITIES AND DIFFERENCES

Which expression(s) could also be followed by *with*?
What other words could you add to replace those in brackets?

compared to
in contrast to
similar / almost identical to
slightly / completely different from
(not) as (spacious) as
less (modern, luxurious) than
in a similar position to / different position from
... has disappeared altogether

Student A

Look at the picture on the right-hand side. It is the inside of the bank where the robbery mentioned in 2.0 took place and it has recently been modernized. Describe the layout and facilities to your partner, commenting on how you think the modernization has improved the interior of the bank. You can use some of the expressions on the Function File card to help you describe the bank.

Student B

Look at the picture on the left-hand side. It is a picture of the same bank, where the robbery took place, but the sketch was drawn before the bank was modernized. After your partner has finished describing the bank on the right-hand side, explain how your picture is similar or different using some of the expressions on the Function File card.

Module 1B • Speaking

2.2 🎧 Extracting recycled information
The bank robbery

Listen only once to a news bulletin describing the bank robbery mentioned in 2.0 and 2.1 and fill in the missing information on the crime report sheet. Then compare your answers in small groups.

ROBBERY AT THE NATIONAL SAVINGS BANK

Location of bank: _____

Time of robbery: _____ *Number of suspects:* _____

Other customers saw a woman giving something to _____

Amount stolen: _____ *Alarm raised by* _____

Gang escaped in _____

2.3 🎤 Identifying word stress

These groups of words appeared in the news bulletin. Read them aloud and try to mark the stresses.

the Nátional Sávings Bánk

Then listen again to the tape and check your answers.

1 an armed robbery
2 a security firm
3 the High Street bank
4 machine guns
5 their afternoon delivery
6 the security guards
7 the bank clerks
8 the alarm button
9 a getaway car
10 double yellow lines
11 a traffic warden
12 a parking ticket

3.0 🎤 Describing, comparing and contrasting
Before and after an explosion

14

People and places • **Module 1B**

Look at the two pictures of a city centre before and after an explosion. In pairs, discuss what the city centre looked like the morning before and the morning after the explosion.

3.1 🎤 Reporting an event in the news

In the same pairs, prepare a one-minute news item about the explosion to be read out on the radio. You could include:

- what is not yet known.
- what is thought to have happened, e.g. a gas leak.
- who was / were injured.
- what was / were smashed or shattered.
- what was disrupted.

Now read out your news item paying attention to the timing of the item, and the strong and weak stresses on the words you use.

🎤 Exam practice: describe, speculate and identify

Identity parade

On pages 113 and 124 there are two sets of people taking part in an identity parade to see if members of the public can identify the thieves, a man and a woman, in a robbery they witnessed.

Student A

Look at the set of pictures on page 113. Choose one man and one woman from each set and describe them in as much detail as possible, saying why you think these two people must be the ones you saw committing the crime. You have one minute to do this.

Student B

Look at the set of pictures on page 124. They are the same as your partner's but they are in a different order. Listen carefully to your partner's descriptions and decide which two people your partner described.

There are more Paper 5 Part 2 tasks in the Task bank on pages 88–91.

Module 1C/D • Speaking

1C/D Jobs and training

Spotlight on Paper 5 Parts 3 and 4

1.0 🎤 **Exchanging opinions**

Too young or too old?
Work through the Function File cards before doing the activity opposite.

GIVING YOUR OPINION

Which expression sounds rather rude and off-hand and suggests that you have nothing else to say?
Which expresses a very strong opinion?

In my opinion / view . . .
Generally speaking, I think . . .
Personally, I haven't the faintest idea about / whether . . .
To my mind . . .
I'd just like to say . . .
As far as I'm concerned . . .
I'm quite convinced that . . .
To be quite honest / frank . . .
If you ask me . . .

ASKING FOR THE OPINION OF OTHERS

Which expression is often used when addressing a group of people in a more formal situation, e.g. a meeting?
Which expressions are often used when addressing an individual in a more formal situation, e.g. a TV interview with a politician?
Which expressions are more suitable for an informal exchange of ideas?

What / How about you?
Would you care to comment on . . . ?
Any comments?
Would you agree with that?
What are your views on . . . ?
What's your opinion?
What do you think . . . ?

Jobs and training • Module 1C/D

Exam hint

You must, of course, state your own point of view but you will also be given credit for inviting your fellow candidates to express their views and encouraging them to make a contribution when they remain silent.

In small groups discuss which of these jobs could be done more successfully by someone in the 20–30 age range or an older person and why. Refer to the Function File cards.

Appoint one person to make a note of the group's opinions and when you have finished, compare your ideas with those of another group.

1.1 🎤 Expressing personal preferences

In pairs ask your partners which of the jobs in the pictures above they would prefer and why. Refer to this Function File card to reply.

EXPRESSING PREFERENCES

Which expression sounds as if it is simply contrasting one thing with another but is actually denoting a very strong preference?
Which expression is more colloquial and would be used in an informal conversation?

I'd much rather (do) . . . than . . .
I could never do / be . . . but I'd really enjoy . . .
There's no comparison between . . . and . . .
I'd prefer . . . to . . .
I'd be far happier doing . . . than . . .
Give me . . . any time!

Module 1C/D • Speaking

2.0 🎤 Asking about personal details

When you go for an interview or apply for a job you may be asked some questions about yourself, your qualifications and experience. You are sometimes asked to produce a Curriculum Vitae (CV) outlining this information.

Use the simplified CV below to ask a partner questions which may be asked in an interview. Make brief notes about your partner.

First name(s): _____ Family name: _____ Date of birth: _____

Address: _____

Education: _____

_____

Qualifications: _____

Experience: _____

Interests / hobbies: _____

_____

Tell the class two things which you found interesting about your partner.

2.1 🎧 Listening for facts and figures

Exam hint

Sometimes information for an answer appears at a later stage on the tape or clarifies what has been said earlier. Pencil in what you hear first, then listen carefully a second time to check your original answer.

Now listen to a radio programme about a man who, as a teenager, was a genius. Fill in the missing details and answer the questions about him.

Name: Dr Simon Marlow   Age: 32

At present: Assistant professor of (1) _____ at the University of (2) _____

1978 Gained (3) _____ passes at Advanced Level

1978–1981 Studied (4) _____ at Essex University

1981–1986 Doctorate in (5) _____ at Oxford

1986 After completing doctorate went to (6) _____

Thinks people should be allowed to specialize in subjects they (7) _____

Weakness: Not very good at (8) _____

What prompted Simon's decision to move in 1986? How do you know? How does he keep in touch with his friends?

2.2 🎤 Sound discrimination

The left-hand words in each pair below all appeared in the interview in 2.1. In pairs, take it in turns to read out one pair of words paying particular attention to the pronunciation and word stress, then discuss the differences in meaning.

1	rewards	rewords	6	vague	vogue
2	drain	grain	7	belief	believe
3	edge	hedge	8	rejected	dejected
4	recalling	recoiling	9	resist	persist
5	pure	poor	10	mail	nail

Jobs and training • Module 1C/D

2.3 🎧 Sound discrimination

Listen to a conversation between a father and his son. Each sentence of their conversation contains one of the words in 2.2 opposite. As you listen to them talking, circle the word you hear.

Exam hint

Listen carefully to the context. A clear idea of the context of what you are listening to and who might be speaking will help you to make a reasoned guess as to any ambiguous words or information.

3.0 🎤 Disagreeing politely

> **DISAGREEING POLITELY**
>
> Which expressions sound as if they are being used to dismiss the other person's point of view?
> Which expressions are more diplomatic?
>
> *There may be some truth in what you say but don't you think it's more a question of . . .?*
> *You must be joking!*
> *I take your point but that's not the way I see it.*
> *Yes, but don't you think that . . .?*
> *I see what you mean but I'm not at all convinced that . . .*
> *True, but I'm afraid I disagree (with) . . .*
> *You can't be serious!*
> *Perhaps, but I can't help thinking that . . .*

Exam hint

You do not have to agree with your fellow-candidates all the time. In fact you will be able to make a fuller contribution to the speaking test if you have some different ideas of your own to express. However, it is not a good idea to indulge in an over-heated argument: most examiners do not want to hear a violent disagreement, which could be embarrassing! So try to be polite and friendly at all times!

Look at these various methods of learning and training and in groups of four discuss which you consider to be the most and the least effective ways of learning or training to do something. Two students should put forward arguments for the options on the top and the other two for those on the bottom. Refer to the Function File cards on page 16 as well as the one above.

Module 1C/D • Speaking

3.1 🎤 Admitting that you might be mistaken

> **ADMITTING THAT YOU MIGHT BE MISTAKEN**
>
> Which expression sounds rather defeatist and is used to end an argument?
> Which expression is very colloquial and rather grudgingly concedes that the other person has a point?
> Which expressions are used to suggest that you might possibly have made a mistake?
> Which expression admits quite freely that you were wrong?
>
> ---
>
> *I hadn't thought of . . . in that way.*
> *Fair enough!*
> *Come to think of it you might be right.*
> *All right – you win!*
> *I must admit it's true that . . .*
> *I suppose you're right.*
> *You're quite right, of course.*

Take the roles you took in 3.0, but this time tell your partners that you have been persuaded by their arguments and say why.

3.2 🎤 Discussion

UNEMPLOYED FIGURES RISE AGAIN

Here's how we solve the unemployment problem!

Why are so many people without work nowadays?
What can we do about it?

In small groups discuss the newspaper headlines and the questions below. You have four to five minutes to reach agreement. Refer to the Function File cards opposite. Appoint a 'secretary' to makes notes on the group's opinions. Remember to invite the other members of the group to have a turn if they remain silent or have not had the opportunity to make a contribution to the conversation.

You might consider:

- the types of jobs available.
- modern methods of production.
- part-time and shift work.
- training / education given to young people.
- retraining given to older people.
- the school-leaving age.
- the age of retirement.
- numbers of people in the world.

Jobs and training • **Module 1C/D**

Exam hint

If your mind goes blank, don't be an empty-headed candidate! Start talking about people or situations you are familiar with, opinions in books or articles you have read, or discuss what you have talked about in class. However, remember what you say **must** be spontaneous and relevant to the discussion. It must not appear to be a prepared speech!

COMMENTING ON SOMETHING YOU KNOW NOTHING ABOUT

Which expression could suggest that you are about to criticize someone or something?
Which expressions sound off-hand and fail to develop the interaction? What effect does using expressions like these have on the person you are talking to?
Why is it a good thing to make an effort to develop the interaction even if you have no opinions on the subject?

Actually, I don't have any first-hand experience of . . . but . . .
Search me!
Personally, I've never had anything to do / had very little to do with . . . but . . .
I have a sneaking suspicion that . . .
Haven't a clue!
It's rather difficult to say but I would imagine . . .

FINDING OUT IF EVERYONE AGREES

Which expression sounds rather dismissive and very informal?
Which sounds rather formal for this kind of discussion?
Which expressions could be used diplomatically to draw a discussion to a close?

So we're agreed on . . .
It looks as if we all agree that . . .
Can I take it that everyone agrees that . . . ?
Are we all in agreement?
It would appear that we are in complete agreement.
Well, that's that then!
We appear to agree on . . .

Each group's secretary can now report back to the class on the group's decisions.

Module 1C/D • Speaking

🎤 Exam practice

The right person for the right job

Part 3

Look at the five photographs of people who are trying to find a job. Their personal interests are illustrated in the thought bubbles. Read the brief notes about them and in small groups decide what kind of job you think would suit these people and why. Take three to four minutes then report your conclusions to the rest of the class.

1 school leaver
   no exam qualification
   no job experience

2 no university degree
   office skills
   willing to work long hours

3 university degree
   no job experience
   easy-going

4 university degree
   three children
   unable to work unsocial hours

5 good administrative skills
   hard worker
   recently made redundant

Part 4

At this point the examiner will join the discussion, asking questions like these. In the same groups discuss the questions.

Why do some people find job interviews so terrifying?
What do you think employers are looking for when they interview people?
What advice would you give to someone going for their first job interview?
What advice would you give to someone who has just failed a job interview?

There are more Paper 5 Part 3 and 4 tasks in the Task bank on pages 91–95.

2 LISTENING

A Sorry, I didn't quite catch that!
B Leisure activities and holidays
C Mind over matter
D Today's technology

2A Sorry, I didn't quite catch that!

Spotlight on Paper 4 Part 1

1.0 🎧 **Identifying background sounds**

> SPECULATING ABOUT WHAT YOU HEAR
>
> What words or phrases would you use to follow the first three expressions? Could you add some alternative expressions to this list?
>
> *It sounds . . .*
> *It sounds like . . .*
> *It sounds as if . . .*
> *I can't make out what it is.*
> *It could very well be / couldn't possibly be . . .*

Exam hint

You will not need to identify background sounds in the exam but they can sometimes be useful clues when trying to put what you hear into a context.

Listen to ten background sounds and, in groups, suggest where you might hear them.

1 _____
2 _____
3 _____
4 _____
5 _____
6 _____
7 _____
8 _____
9 _____
10 _____

Module 2A • Listening

1.1 🎧 Coping with voices against background sounds.

You will hear six people talking over some background sounds. In groups, decide who might be speaking, what the background sound is, where the person might be and what might have happened or might be happening. Try to use some of the expressions on the Function File card in 1.0.

	Speaker	Sound	Place	Situation
1				
2				
3				
4				
5				
6				

2.0 🎧 Coping with accents

Exam hint

Try not to be put off by accents. They are used in the exam only because not everyone speaks English with the same accent. You will almost certainly be exposed to a variety of accents in the exam but they are never unintelligible – and you will never be asked to identify them!

You will hear five speakers with different accents. As you listen, try to match the speakers' accents with the nationalities below. There are some clues in what the speakers are saying to help you! Then compare your answers with a partner's.

a American   c English   e Irish   g South African
b Australian   d Scottish   f Welsh

Speaker 1 _____   Speaker 4 _____

Speaker 2 _____   Speaker 5 _____

Speaker 3 _____

2.1 🎧 Making a logical guess about context

Listen to five speakers and try to work out what they might be talking about. Make some brief notes in the spaces below.

1 _____
2 _____
3 _____
4 _____
5 _____

Which key words helped you to guess the context?

1 _____
2 _____
3 _____
4 _____
5 _____

3.0 🎧 Keeping an open mind about what you hear

FINDING OUT ABOUT CORRECT SPELLING

Which expressions would you use to decide with a partner whether these words are spelt correctly or not?

a acommodation   h decieve
b conscience   i courteous
c benefited   j guarantee
d professional   k wether
e gauge   l busness
f embarrasment   m feasible
g comparable   n accustomed

How do you spell 'fair', you know, 'blond'?
Do you spell '. . .' with one 'c' or two?
Are there two 't's in '. . .'?
Have I spelt this correctly?
Could you please check my spelling of '. . .'?
Is '. . .' spelt with 'ie' or 'ei'?

You will hear twelve words on tape. As you listen, write them in the spaces below. There are two ways, if not more, of spelling the words!

e.g. *fare* (payment to travel)
      fair (not raining, blond, just, entertainment with stalls and rides)

'Have I got the right fare?'

1 _____
2 _____
3 _____

Module 2A • Listening

4 _____
5 _____
6 _____
7 _____
8 _____
9 _____
10 _____
11 _____
12 _____

Now compare your answers with those of a partner and decide what the words mean.

3.1

Exam hint

Although no exercise in Paper 4 tests spelling alone, spelling is taken into consideration in the marking of the paper as a wrong spelling can interfere with communication. You may have to use your knowledge of spelling rules to make a logical guess about how to spell a word.

🎤 Recognizing words

Read out the words below and in pairs decide whether they follow any common spelling patterns. You may need to refer back to exercise 4.0 on page 9.

1 rat   rate
2 write   written
3 conceit   believe
4 through   rough   thorough
5 knowledgeable   receivable   noticeable
6 elf   elves / belief   beliefs
7 potato   potatoes / piano   pianos
8 fry   frying
9 exceed   exist
10 quarrel   quarrelled
11 academy   accommodation
12 mile   mileage

Give other examples which follow each of the patterns.

4.0

🎧 Interpreting information correctly

You will hear a news item from local radio then you will hear the item again split into ten short extracts. The notes, jotted down while the writer was listening to the news item, are incorrect as the writer has misheard what the speaker said. Listen carefully to the complete news item first, then to each extract and try to correct the notes.

1 . . . Ronald Broom . . .
2 . . . 1906 . . . 1918 . . .
3 . . . five teas . . .
4 . . . owned black taxis . . .
5 . . . proper tea . . .
6 . . . disclosure . . .
7 . . . guess right . . .
8 . . . the grand four . . . free storage   . . . down-and-out
9 . . . untaxed . . .
10 . . . ferry across . . .   it's some fare . . .

Sorry, I didn't quite catch that! • **Module 2A**

4.1 🎤 Evaluating differences

A This is a picture of the kind of shop mentioned in 4.0. Describe either the right or the left side of the picture to a partner.

B Now join with another pair and discuss the positive and/or negative aspects of a shop like the one above, of present-day supermarkets and of open-air markets.

You might consider:

- the type of service
- prices
- choice of goods
- time available for shopping
- location of shop / market

Allow three or four minutes. Appoint one member of the group to take notes. When you have finished, report your decisions to the rest of the class.

27

Exam practice: sentence completion

You will hear a news story about a man who made newspaper headlines because of his metal detector. As you listen, complete the sentences. If you don't recognize some of the words you need, try to guess the spelling! You will hear the recording twice.

Mr Lawson works as a (1)_____.

His discovery had lain undetected since (2)_____.

He stored his treasure in (3)_____.

The discovery was made on (4)_____.

After his discovery, he immediately (5)_____.

If he does not comply with the request of the authorities, he faces (6)_____.

Mr Lawson found the treasure while searching for lost (7)_____.

He will not receive compensation for objects he did not himself (8)_____.

He thinks that in future people with metal detectors might be unwilling to (9)_____.

In the last few years metal-detecting has resulted in the handing in of (10)_____.

David Gurney thinks that people who make these discoveries should be (11)_____.

Perhaps now we should think about changing (12)_____.

There are more Paper 4 Part 1 tasks in the Task bank on pages 96–98.

2B Leisure activities and holidays

Spotlight on Paper 4 Part 2

1.0 🎤 Asking for and expressing opinions

In groups of three or four try to name these various activities then check your answers with the key on page 147.

Find out
a if the students in your group have ever tried any of these activities and whether they enjoyed them.
b which of the activities they would really like to try and why.
c which of the activities they would absolutely detest doing and why.

1.1 🎧 Listening for information which is repeated

Exam hint

In the exam you will have time to read through the notes for the task before you listen to the tape. Use the time to read the instructions and notes carefully so that you are well-prepared for what you are going to hear and what you have to do.

Listen to some young people talking about leisure activities. They say the same thing more than once but in a different way, e.g. by using the same words in a different context or different words in the same context, or saying the same thing later. This is called *recycling* information.

As you listen to the speakers, put a tick (✓) beside the activities from 1.0 which are mentioned.

1.2 🎤 Speculating

Exam hint

Do not write too much in the gaps in the note-taking task – about one to three words. The space will tell you roughly how much you are expected to write. You may need to rephrase your information slightly to fit a different context, e.g. 'He is a second-year university student.' *He is in* **his** / **the second year** *at university*.

Look at the grid below and guess what missing information you will need to supply and what the headings A–D will be.

A	B	C	D
(1)_____	Birmingham	£1 a session	Phone (2)_____
Bird watching	(3)_____	£3 a day	Phone during (4)_____
(5)_____	Bristol	£17 (6)_____	Send (7)_____
Climbing	Southport	(8)_____	Write in
(9)_____	(10)_____	£2.50 a class	Write in

Module 2B • Listening

1.3 🎧 **Extracting and filling in missing information**

Listen to the tape and fill in the missing information in the table in 1.2. Listen only once – all the information you need is recycled in some way.

1.4 🎤 **Making assumptions based on listening material**

Try to answer the following questions about the programme you heard in 1.3. Listen again to the programme if you wish.

a Who do you think the programme is aimed at?
b What style of language does the programme adopt?
c What do you think the presenters look like?
d What kind of people might they be?

2.0 🎧 **Identifying word stress in new vocabulary**

You will hear ten phrases connected with travel and holidays. As you listen, write the phrases in the spaces below. The first is done for you.

1 a package holiday
2 _____
3 _____
4 _____
5 _____
6 _____
7 _____
8 _____
9 _____
10 _____

Identifying word stress helps you to understand what is being said – and using word stress correctly yourself will make what you say more easily understood! Listen again and mark the stresses on the words you have written down, e.g. *a páckage hóliday*, then read them aloud.

2.1 🎧 Identifying repeated information

Listen to a radio advert for a half-price bargain holiday break being offered by a national newspaper. Tick the words and phrases below every time you hear them mentioned or referred to in some way.

a two nights' holiday for the price of one _____
b tokens _____
c the *Daily Telegraph* _____
d between August 14 and September 6 _____
e collector cards _____
f you can take advantage of this offer twice _____

Compare the number of ticks you made with a partner. Which references appeared the most often? Why were these ones repeated so often?

2.2 🎤 Discussing how something is organized

Using the words and phrases in 2.1 discuss briefly with a partner how the bargain break operates. Allow yourselves about two minutes.

3.0 🎧 Identifying paraphrases

Listen to a short extract from the introduction to a travel programme and, as you listen, note down the three phrases which have the same meaning as the following expressions. They are not in the same order as they appear on the tape!

a really enjoying yourself
b using your own means of transport
c forgetting about your everyday worries

3.1 🎧 Interpreting and rephrasing information

Read through the multiple choice questions and the clues which are given to help you focus on the relevant information for the right and wrong answers.

1 What is the difference between 'luggers' and 'tuggers'?
   A 'Luggers' are caravanners whereas 'tuggers' are motorcaravanners.
   B 'Luggers' are motorcaravanners whereas 'tuggers' are caravanners.
   C 'Luggers' and 'tuggers' think there is very little difference between them.

Clues: listen for *are known as*
they have a word for it

2 The programme suggests that caravanners
   A outnumber motorcaravanners.
   B dislike motorcaravanners.
   C tolerate motorcaravanners.

Clues: listen for *well in the minority*
on good terms
a trace of unease

Module 2B • Listening

3 Potential buyers should ask themselves whether
A it would be cheaper to hire a vehicle.
B the vehicle would be too small for camping.
C the vehicle would be too big for everyday use.

Clues: listen for *for an experimental weekend*
family car
it will need to be

4 The luggers' motto could be
A retire early and travel
B ignore the discomfort and travel
C travel in comfort

Clues: listen for *Rick Jenkins who*
while living in
become accustomed to

Exam hint

If you don't recognize a word, don't panic! The word is often explained in a different way later in the listening material and unusual vocabulary items are not tested.

Then listen to someone talking on the same radio programme as you heard in 3.0 about people who own motorcaravans and choose the answer, either **A**, **B** or **C**, which best expresses what the speaker is saying. You will probably need to listen to the tape twice.

3.2   🎤 Advising someone (not) to do something and putting forward another point of view

Pairwork

Student A

Your partner wants to buy a motorcaravan but you do not like motorcaravans. Basing your advice on what you heard in 3.1, advise your partner not to buy one. Before you begin, refer to this Function File card and discuss your answers to the questions with other Student As.

ADVISING SOMEONE (NOT) TO DO SOMETHING

Which expression sounds too impersonal and too formal for this situation?
Which expression sounds very familiar and somewhat offensive?
Which expression sounds very colloquial and suggests some irritation on the part of the speaker?
Which expression implies that the listener has not been doing the right thing up to this point?
How would you complete the sentence *I'd certainly recommend . . .*?
Can you think of any other expressions to add to the list?

If I were you, I'd (wouldn't) . . .
You'd better (not) . . .
On no account should you . . .
You'd be crazy (not) to . . .
Why on earth don't you . . . ?
I think you'd be well advised to . . .
I'd certainly recommend . . .
It's high time you . . .

Function File

Student B
You are very interested in buying a motorcaravan but your partner doesn't like them. Explain to your partner what you think about motorcaravans and say why you think your partner might be wrong about them. Before you begin, refer to this Function File card and discuss your answers to the questions with other Student Bs.

PUTTING FORWARD ANOTHER POINT OF VIEW

Which expressions sound like insults?
Can you add any other expressions to the list?

Yes, but on the other hand, don't you think that . . .
But to look at it from another point of view . . .
Look, nobody in their right mind would think that . . .
Surely you can't really believe . . . ?
But wouldn't you agree that . . . ?

Exam practice: sentence completion

You will hear part of a radio programme which suggests what tourists from all over the world think about each other. For questions 1–10, complete the sentences with an appropriate word or short phrase. **Listen very carefully as you will hear this recording ONCE only.**

Some German tourists rise early to reserve a (1)_____.

All nations have their own ideas about (2)_____.

The Germans think many Dutch tourists (3)_____.

The Spaniards think the Dutch and Belgians are not very

good at driving (4)_____.

French tourists in other countries never seem to enjoy (5)_____.

In restaurants the British never (6)_____.

The Italians love to visit (7)_____.

The Americans make a big effort to be (8)_____.

The Japanese are never seen without (9)_____.

It seems as if the whole world is slowly becoming (10)_____.

There are more Paper 4 Part 2 tasks in the Task bank on pages 98–100.

Module 2C • Listening

2C Mind over matter

Spotlight on Paper 4 Part 3

1.0 🎧 Listening for unusual information

Exam hint

Although the listening passage may be about something you are not very familiar with, and the task may look rather complicated at first sight, do not panic! There will always be enough information on the tape and on your answer sheet for you to understand what it is about and do what is expected of you.

Memory mapping

Listen to someone talking about memory mapping and complete the sentences. The capital letters in 2–8 are the first letters of words in lists of information which are often difficult to remember.

There is only one word in the dictionary beginning with the letters (1)_____.

The letters ROYGBIV help us remember the (2)_____.

SMHEO help us remember the (3)_____.

CANT help us remember the (4)_____.

WIMNM help us remember the (5)_____.

In the COrner reminds us where (6)_____ is.

On the EqUAtOR reminds us where 7)_____ is.

BP reminds us of two countries without (8)_____.

A successful aid to memory mapping always has a strong (9)_____.

1.1 🎧 Making notes while you listen

Exam hint

Practise writing as you hear the information, but at the same time keep listening to what comes next. If you hesitate, you may miss vital information for the next question. Practise in your own language by trying to take notes from the news on the radio or TV using a kind of 'shorthand' or note form of your own. You will soon learn how to do it quite quickly!

Memory mapping

Listen to the tape again and note down the words that the capital letters in 1.0 can stand for. Try to write down as much as you can without having to stop the tape.

1 ROYGBIV = _____   4 WIMNM = _____

2 SMHEO = _____   5 BP = _____

3 CANT = _____

1.2 🎤 Design your own mnemonics

In small groups can you make up mnemonics for the items below?

a the countries of North-West Africa: Algeria, Morocco, Tunisia
b the countries of the White Nile: Egypt, Sudan, Uganda

Can you think of mnemonics in English for other things you find difficult to remember?

Mind over matter • Module 2C

2.0 🎧 Listening for key information

Exam hint

Try to work out what the important or key words are to help you focus on what to listen for as you read through statements or multiple choice options.

You will hear someone talking to an author about two of her books.

A Before you listen read the statements carefully and notice how the important information in 1–4 is highlighted in **bold**. What words would you highlight in 5–7?

1 Deborah's **first book** highlights the differences between the way **young and old people speak**.
2 Deborah's **second book** reminds us how easy it is for **communication to break down**.
3 The **question-and-answer** technique **prevents** us from appearing **too vague**.
4 **Men** often ask **too many personal questions**.
5 The British are happier using a person's first name.
6 Americans like being asked personal questions.
7 You should analyse your own style of speaking carefully.

B Now listen for the information targeted in **bold** and decide whether the speaker makes these statements or not.

2.1 🎤 Correcting what is not accurate

In pairs correct the statements in 2.0 which are not accurate, using expressions on this Function File card.

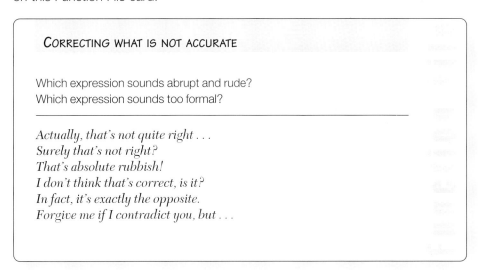

> CORRECTING WHAT IS NOT ACCURATE
>
> Which expression sounds abrupt and rude?
> Which expression sounds too formal?
>
> ---
>
> *Actually, that's not quite right . . .*
> *Surely that's not right?*
> *That's absolute rubbish!*
> *I don't think that's correct, is it?*
> *In fact, it's exactly the opposite.*
> *Forgive me if I contradict you, but . . .*

3.0 🎧 Listening for key information in multiple choice questions

A You will hear part of a radio programme about how to communicate with people. Before you listen, read through the multiple choice questions. The key information in 1 and 2 is highlighted in **bold**. Highlight what you consider to be the key information in 3 and 4.

1 Conversation is a tool used by
 A **men** and **women** for the **same purpose**.
 B **women** to **maintain** a **relationship**.
 C **men** to **create connections** between people.
 D **men** and **women** to **create** a **sense** of **community**.

Module 2C • Listening

2 When a cake shop owner asked her male manager to do something, he
   A **forgot** all about doing it.
   B **refused** to do it.
   C **decided** he hadn't time to do it.
   D **quarrelled** with her about doing it.

3 When a mother asked her adult son, who had a full-time job, to contribute to the household expenses, what did he do?
   A He rented a place of his own.
   B He reluctantly agreed to pay rent.
   C He pretended he had not heard her.
   D He left the matter open.

4 What is the difference between girls' and boys' conversational styles?
   A Boys give girls direct commands.
   B Girls get their own way by making suggestions.
   C Boys give each other options when deciding what to do.
   D Girls are more likely to be assertive than boys.

B Now listen to the tape and put a pencil mark beside the most likely answer. Then, referring back to the Function File card in 2.1, tell a partner why you think the other options are not correct. When you have finished, listen to the tape again to check that your answers are correct.

3.1 A breakdown in communication

The following two exchanges appeared on the tape in 3.0. What breakdown of communication took place?

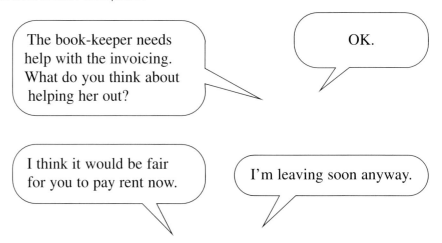

3.2 Listening for key information in multiple choice questions

A You will hear a continuation of the radio programme about how to communicate with people. Before you listen, read through the multiple choice questions below and highlight what **you** consider to be the key information in the options.

1 How should the cake shop owner give orders to the male employee?
   A Insist that he helps with the invoicing.
   B Politely tell him exactly what she wants him to do.
   C Persuade him over a period of time to do what she wants.
   D Ask him directly why he won't do what she asks.

2 How should the mother deal with her son?
   A Insist that he honours her wishes.
   B Encourage him to be more honest with her.
   C Give him a deadline to produce the money.
   D Ask him directly when she can expect a contribution.

B Listen to the tape and put a pencil mark beside the most likely answer, then, again using the Function File card in 2.1, tell a partner why you think the other options are not correct.

Now listen again and check that you have chosen the right answer.

🎧 Exam practice: multiple choice questions

Listen to two people, Susan and Dave, talking about how to communicate with each other and, as you listen, choose the correct option from **A**, **B**, **C** or **D**. You will hear the recording twice.

(Remember, before you listen, read through the multiple choice questions and options. Highlight the key information to listen for and do not make your final choice of answer until you have heard the whole piece twice.)

1 What initial statement does Susan make about men's and women's speaking styles?
   A Both men and women mix 'business' and 'personal' conversation.
   B Women think personal conversation helps working relationships.
   C Men think personal conversation helps them to conduct business.
   D Women think personal conversation inappropriate when talking to men.

2 According to Susan, what should a woman who works with men try to do?
   A Never socialize with colleagues after work.
   B Keep the 'small talk' for breaks at work.
   C Never ask very personal questions.
   D Avoid becoming involved with colleagues.

3 What mistake did one woman editor make?
   A She indulged in too much 'small talk' with her female employees.
   B She delegated too much work to the other employees.
   C She appointed another manager to run the office.
   D She underestimated the importance of the personal touch.

4 How did the woman editor rectify her mistake?
   A She decided to recruit more male employees.
   B She took on more responsibility herself.
   C She modified a decision she had previously made.
   D She allowed the other employees longer breaks during the day.

5 What final comment does Susan make?
   A You should get the balance right.
   B She doesn't know how to solve the problem easily.
   C We would be better off separating the sexes.
   D Whatever you do, you can't win.

There are more Paper 4 Part 3 tasks in the Task bank on pages 100–104.

Module 2D • Listening

2D Today's technology

Spotlight on Paper 4 Part 4

1.0 🎤 **Finding out a partner's opinion**

Commenting on something you may know nothing about

In pairs, ask your partner to think of one good and one bad point about video games, then, with the rest of the class, put a list of good and bad points on the board.

1.1 🎤 **Interpreting visual information**

In the same pairs as in 1.0, look at the three pie charts and try to explain what they are showing.

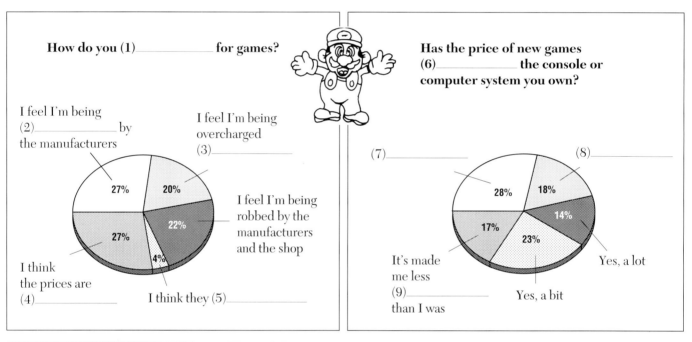

How do you (1) _____ for games?

- I feel I'm being (2) _____ by the manufacturers — 27%
- I feel I'm being overcharged (3) _____ — 20%
- I feel I'm being robbed by the manufacturers and the shop — 22%
- I think they (5) _____ — 4%
- I think the prices are (4) _____ — 27%

Has the price of new games (6) _____ the console or computer system you own?

- (7) _____ — 28%
- (8) _____ — 18%
- Yes, a lot — 14%
- Yes, a bit — 23%
- It's made me less (9) _____ than I was — 17%

Exam hint

Don't be put off by an unusual layout or format in an examination task, e.g. diagrams and charts. Keep calm and just work out what information is being asked for.

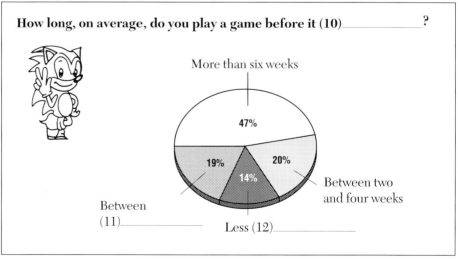

How long, on average, do you play a game before it (10) _____ ?

- More than six weeks — 47%
- Between two and four weeks — 20%
- Less (12) _____ — 14%
- Between (11) _____ — 19%

38

Today's technology • Module 2D

1.2 🎧 Listening for specific information
Facts and figures

You will hear some young people answering questions about video games. As you listen, fill in the missing information in the charts in 1.1. Remember that you may have to rephrase some of the information you hear.

Compare your answers with a partner. Which answers needed changing or putting into a different context?

2.0 🎧 Interpreting attitudes
The pros and cons of video games

Listen to some people talking about video games and decide whether their statements indicate that they approve or disapprove of or are neutral towards the games by ticking (✓) the appropriate box.

	Approve	Disapprove	Neutral
1			
2			
3			
4			
5			
6			
7			
8			
9			

2.1 🎧 Identifying speakers
Making assumptions about identity

Now listen again and decide who might be making these statements. More than one option may be possible but here one of the options is not used at all.

	Parent	Teenager	Policeman	Doctor	Video manufacturer
1					
2					
3					
4					
5					
6					
7					
8					
9					

Exam hint

The ability to make a logical assumption about identity will help you in Part 4 of Paper 4. Listen for clues like 'our games', 'my children', 'our patients', 'I can't stop', 'order replacements', which will help you to decide who the speaker might be. Remember – in the exam not all the alternatives are needed to answer the question!

Which words helped you to guess the identity of the speakers?

Module 2D • Listening

2.2 🎧 Sound discrimination

Words which sound similar but have different meanings can be misleading in a listening test. It is important to be able to identify a word in a context. Read out the groups of words in the table below and guess which words (one from each group) you might hear when listening to some young people talking about their reactions to video games.

1 consul	console	consultation
2 strictly	sickly	thickly
3 violet	violate	violent
4 conducted	conducive	conductor
5 lightning	frightening	fighting
6 burrow	barrow	borrow

Now listen to the tape and circle the word in each group which you hear. The words appear in the order in which they occur on the tape.

2.3 🎧 Matching information

Attitudes of players

Read through the information below carefully then listen to a longer version of what you heard in 2.2 and match the information to the speaker. In this exercise each option is used just once, and there is only one option that is not used at all. You may have to listen twice.

Neill Moore

1 ____

2 ____

3 ____

4 ____

Khim Karaud

5 ____

6 ____

Jaspal Bhatti

7 ____

Nicholas Scott

8 ____

9 ____

10 ____

a doesn't talk to people any more
b gets bored at home
c plays for half an hour
d neglects homework
e received the game as a present
f favourite game is Street Fighter 2
g borrows aggressive games
h plays for up to five hours
i thinks some games are boring
j likes playing more than watching TV
k does homework before playing

Which option is not used?

Exam hint

When looking at a multiple matching exercise underline, either mentally or with a pencil, what you consider to be the key words in the options. This will reduce the memory load and help you to skim read all the options and identify the one you need. Remember also to read and listen to the instructions carefully both on your exam paper and on the tape.

3.0 🎤 Anticipating what you are going to hear

Questionnaire

Read through the possible answers to a questionnaire about watching TV. The questionnaire requires you to tick one answer for questions 2–7 and one or more for questions 1 and 8. In pairs, decide what the questions might be.

1 _____?
- a a television
- b a video recorder
- c a satellite dish
- d cable TV

2 _____?
- a not at all
- b once or twice
- c frequently

3 _____?
- a Pause for a moment just to see what's on.
- b Stand with your nose pressed against the window.
- c Walk straight past.

4 _____?
- a gripping
- b compelling if you're in the mood
- c to be avoided

5 _____?
- a Yes.
- b No.
- c Make it about £500,000 and I'll think about it.

6 _____?
- a Ring your friends and ask if you can go round and watch with them.
- b Get out a book or switch on the radio.
- c Feel as if the world has ended.

7 _____?
- a TV has killed the art of conversation.
- b Judicious TV viewing can be educational and entertaining.
- c People should be quiet when the TV's on.

8 _____?
- a eating
- b reading
- c taking exercise

Module 2D • Listening

3.1 🎧 Listening for specific information

Exam hint

Remember, if you find it difficult to write notes as you listen, develop a kind of 'shorthand' – abbreviations you will be able to understand when you look at your notes again, for example
∵ = because of, → = leading to,
f = female, m = male,
smth = something,
smb = somebody.

Questions

Listen to the questions for the questionnaire in 3.0 and makes notes in the spaces provided above. As you are focusing on listening skills, you do not need to write a perfectly constructed sentence, just the key information. You do, however, need to pay particular attention to spelling.

How did the questions compare with yours?

3.2 🎤 Evaluating the results

An addict or not?

Do the questionnaire in 3.0. Choose the answer which best sums up your feelings and attitudes, then check your scores on the answers to the questionnaire on page 148 in the key and find out whether you really are an addict or not!

Do you agree with the assessment? Why? Why not?

🎧 Exam practice: multiple matching

You will hear various people talking about today's technology. You will hear the recording twice. The first time you hear the recording you should do task one. The second time, do task two. Listen carefully for the key words, like the ones highlighted in 2.1, which will give you clues as to identity and context.

Task one

Match the extracts as you hear them with the people listed A–H.

Exam hint

In the exam you will only need five out of the eight options. Do not try to use them all just because they are there – though you must consider all the options when making your choice!

A social worker	1
B parent	
C shop assistant	2
D student	
E teacher	3
F actor	4
G film producer	
H doctor	5

Task two

Match the extracts as you hear them with the technology listed A–H.

A video films	
B TV	6
C radio	7
D video games	
E personal stereo	8
F computer	9
G compact discs	
H mobile phone	10

There are more Paper 4 Part 4 tasks in the Task bank on pages 104–107.

3 SPEAKING

A What if . . . ?

B Yesterday and today

C/D Art and culture

3A What if . . .?

Spotlight on Paper 5 Part 1

1.0 🎤 **Predictions about your own future**

> **TALKING ABOUT CERTAINTY, POSSIBILITY AND IMPROBABILITY**
>
> Which expressions would you use to express near certainty, possibility or improbability?
> What structures follow each of the expressions?
> Could you add any other expressions to the list?
>
> *I doubt whether . . .*
> *I'm bound to . . .*
> *There's a fairly good chance of . . .*
> *There's no doubt in my mind whatsoever that . . .*
> *I shouldn't be surprised if . . .*
> *I'm absolutely convinced that . . .*
> *There's very little chance of / that . . .*

In pairs, discuss this list of life events and, using the expressions on the Function File card, grade the events A, B or C, according to how likely it is that these things will happen to you.

Life events

- have twins ___
- live to be 100 years old ___
- become a great-grandparent ___
- enjoy your job ___
- travel into outer space ___
- be made redundant ___
- become rich and famous ___
- live alone for a number of years ___
- be happy ___
- change your outlook on life ___

A = almost certain

B = possible

C = improbable

Module 3A • Speaking

2.0 Past predictions about the future

> **INTERPRETING PAST IDEAS**
>
> Which expression sounds formal and rather impersonal?
> Can you add any expressions to the list?
>
> *They obviously thought cities would / might . . .*
> *It is reasonable to assume they thought life would / might . . .*
> *Apparently they were convinced teachers would / could . . .*
> *Presumably they imagined transport would / might . . .*

Exam hint

Remember to stick to a more complex sentence structure (*they thought cities would . . .*), once you have started using it. Do not forget what you are saying and lapse into an inappropriate simple sentence structure (*they think cities will*). The examiner will be listening to see what level of vocabulary and grammar you are capable of using effectively. You don't want your use of the more complex structure to seem like a lucky guess!

These pictures were published many years ago. They show what people thought life would be like in the future, i.e. our 'today' (or even 'yesterday'!), and what it would be like in the more distant future.

In pairs, taking each picture in turn, decide when the pictures might have been published and how they represent what people thought the future would be like. Use the expressions on the Function File card.

'the teacher of the future'

'the street of the future'

'the city of the future'

44

What if . . . ? • **Module 3A**

2.1 🎤 **Comparing past predictions with future predictions**

In groups of three or four, discuss how the pictures in 2.0 compare with life as it is today and think of ideas about what it might be like in the future. Discuss which ideas are or might be similar to, and which different from, the artists' impressions in 2.0.

3.0 🎧 **Hypothesizing**

You will hear a radio presenter talking about a forthcoming radio programme called *What if . . .?* Read through the statements below then, as you listen, decide whether the presenter makes the statements or not by writing Y (for yes) or N (for no) beside them.

1. The programme is the last in the series.
2. *What if . . .?* is about events in the future.
3. It is an outside broadcast.
4. The programme is speculating about a military crisis.
5. It is speculating about a country carrying out a threat.
6. It mentions the danger of underestimating an opponent's strength.

3.1 🎤 **Variable stress**

The words on the left all appeared on the tape in 3.0. They are stressed differently from the words on the right. Read them all aloud and mark the stresses.

e.g. *to presént   présence*

1 final	finality	5 actually	actuality
2 historical	history	6 calculated	calculation
3 apocalyptic	apocalypse	7 retaliation	retaliate
4 capability	capable		

Now use one word from each pair in a sentence of your own, spoken to a partner.

3.2 🎤 **Speculating about the past**

In groups of three, take it in turns to ask **and answer** one of the following questions using *. . . would have (done), if . . . had (done)*.

1. What (happen) if the 1962 Cuban missile crisis (teeter) over the edge?
2. What (happen) if the US (carry out) its threat to bomb the Soviet missile sites?
3. What (happen) if subsequent retaliation (take place)?

Now ask and answer similar questions about what would or wouldn't have happened in the past *if . . .* Remember, you need to talk about the opposite of what actually happened!

4. mankind / invent the wheel
5. dinosaurs / be wiped out
6. the whole human race / become vegetarian
7. penicillin / be discovered
8. other animals / develop the same intelligence as human beings

Module 3A • Speaking

4.0 🎤 Speculating about the future

What will *you* be doing in 20 years' time?
Tell a partner what you think you'll be doing in 20 years' time. Use some of the expressions on the Function File card on page 43.

Exam hint
Remember to reply saying what you'll be doing, where you'll be living, etc. This will show that you have listened carefully to the question and are capable of using more sophisticated language.

4.1 🎧 Listening for specific information

The picture below was used in an advertisement for a Life Insurance and Pensions company.

The advertisement also appeared on the radio and TV. Read through the notes below then, as you listen to the advertisement, fill in the missing information.

Sun Alliance
Life and Pensions
Company promise: sizeable (1) _____ in year 2010.
On application for quotation, free (2) _____
At the start of plan: free (3) _____
If you (4) _____, free weekend accommodation for two.
Bonuses: depend on (5) _____
Company promise: keep ahead of (6) _____

4.2 🎤 Discussing effectiveness

In small groups, decide:
- whether the advertisement is an effective way of selling people life insurance and persuading them to save money for the future.
- whether or not you would be interested in what the company is offering and why.
- what you would spend the lump sum of money on.

Allow three or four minutes then report your decisions to the rest of the class.

5.0 Expressing wishes and regrets

> **EXPRESSING WISHES AND REGRETS**
>
> Which constructions can be used after these expressions?
> Which seem to be the most expressive?
>
> *If only . . . !*
> *I wish . . .*
> *How I wish . . . !*
> *Had I known what was going to happen, I . . .*

Interpreting artwork

Decide what the people in the drawings might be wishing and why. Use the expressions on the Function File card.

Module 3B • Speaking

5.1 🎤 Talking about your own wishes and regrets

In pairs, find out three things that your partner wishes: one referring to the past, one to the present and one to the future.

> ### 🎤 Exam practice: asking questions
>
> Find a new partner.
> You have three or four minutes to find out some information about each other but you must ask for the information using full questions, e.g. *How long have you been learning English?*
>
> **Student A**
> Turn to page 108 and find out the answers to the information requested on the information card.
>
> **Student B**
> Turn to page 112 and find out the answers to the information requested on the information card.
>
> Now tell the class what you think is the most interesting thing about your partner.

There are more Paper 5 Part 1 tasks in the Task bank on pages 86–88.

3B Yesterday and today

Spotlight on Paper 5 Part 2

1.0 🎤 Describing and spotting the differences

A French Town

On your own, look at these two pictures of the French town Wissant and find two things which are the same and five things which are different.

WISSANT Hier et Aujourd'hui

48

Yesterday and today • **Module 3B**

1.1 🎤 Linking contrasting ideas

> **LINKING CONTRASTING IDEAS**
>
> Which two expressions would be inappropriate for linking contrasting ideas when talking about two pictures?
>
> *whereas*
> *while*
> *although*
> *but*
> *on the other hand*
> *nevertheless*

Groupwork

In pairs, tell another pair of students what similarities and differences you found in 1.0, using the words and expressions above.

1.2 🎤 Giving yourself time to think

> **GIVING YOURSELF TIME TO THINK**
>
> Which of the last four expressions offer:
> - a logical explanation?
> - a possible explanation?
>
> *Er... I would say that...*
> *Well, now, let me see...*
> *It's difficult to say exactly but...*
> *I can't be sure but...*
> *...there might have been...*
> *...there can't have been...*
> *...there must have been...*
> *...there could have been...*

Exam hint

You may need some time to think but don't waste time panicking in your own language! Think aloud in English. Using fillers can often give you the time you need. However, do not overuse them as the examiner might think you are at a loss for words permanently!

In groups of three or four, allow yourselves three or four minutes to decide:
- when the first picture was taken.
- what has happened to the small town since the first picture was taken.

Use the Function File card and think about:
- the number of inhabitants
- the existence of the war memorial
- changes in transport
- lifestyle of the people

Report back to another group on your decisions.

Module 3B • Speaking

2.0 🎤 Describing differences in attitudes

Brighton Beach

Look at the two pictures of people at the beach

In pairs, decide what the time interval between the pictures might be, then prepare a one-minute comparison of the scenes pointing out the possible differences in the *attitudes* of the people in the pictures. Make brief notes to help you remember what you have prepared, if you wish, but remember that in the exam you will be expected to begin talking almost immediately. You could mention their attitudes towards and feelings about:

- modesty
- sunbathing and swimming
- leisure activities
- fashion

Now give your one-minute talk (30 seconds each!) to another pair of students **without looking at any notes you may have made**!

Yesterday and today • **Module 3B**

2.1 🎧 Listening for answers to questions

Exam hint

To help you with note-taking, listen to the news on the radio in your own language and practise jotting down all the relevant news in note form. When you have devised your own note-taking style, try listening to a similar broadcast in English. The news is good training for note-taking as it is packed with facts and figures, names and places, all of which are relevant.

You will hear someone talking on a radio programme about the seaside resort of Brighton as it used to be and as it is today. Read through the following questions then, as you listen, make notes to help you answer them. You may need to listen twice.

1 What happened in 1753?
2 What led to this 'event' happening?
3 What two things did Richard Russell advise people to do?
4 Why did he advise them to do this?
5 Why might his advice not be considered a good thing today?
6 What happened in 1850?
7 Why did this happen?
8 According to the programme, how is Brighton regarded today?

2.2 🎤 Variable stress

The words on the left all appeared on the tape. They are stressed differently from the words on the right. Read them all aloud and mark the stress.

e.g. *pálace   palátial*

1	invented	inventory
2	explained	explanation
3	historic	history
4	publication	publish
5	advantages	advantageous
6	various	variety
7	moderation	moderate
8	magnet	magnetic

Use one word from each pair in a sentence of your own, spoken to a partner.

3.0 Asking someone to repeat something

> **POLITELY ASKING SOMEONE TO REPEAT SOMETHING**
>
> Which expression would you use if a loud background noise interfered with what the speaker was saying?
> Which expression sounds very polite indeed?
> Which expressions are more informal?
> Which expression could sound rather rude?
>
> ---
>
> *I'm sorry, I didn't quite catch that . . .*
> *Sorry – what was that again?*
> *Sorry – could you say that again, please?*
> *Sorry – I couldn't hear what you said.*
> *What did you say?*
> *Could you repeat that, please?*
> *I'm **so** sorry, but I'm not sure I understood correctly.*

Luxury hotel (Groupwork for three students)

Student A
Describe the picture below. As you describe the picture, try to explain what might / could / must have happened to the hotel. Be ready to explain what you have said in a slightly different way if your partner does not seem to understand you.

Students B and C
At intervals interrupt politely (without annoying your partner), pretending that you haven't heard or understood what your partner has said. Use the expressions on the Function File card.

Yesterday and today • **Module 3B**

When you have finished, look at the picture below and suggest what might / could / must have happened to the train.
Student B: describe the picture.
Students A and C: interrupt politely to ask for clarification.

Now change roles again. Student C, describe the picture below, suggesting what might / could / must have happened to the ship.
Students A and B, interrupt politely to ask for clarification.

Module 3B • Speaking

3.1 🎤 Asking if someone agrees

> **ASKING IF SOMEONE AGREES**
>
> Which expression expects the listener to agree?
> Which expression sounds as if you are trying to persuade someone to agree with you?
> Which expression gives the impression that you do not believe what you are hearing?
>
> ---
>
> *Do / Would you agree with . . . ?*
> *You agree, don't you?*
> *I wonder if you would agree . . .*
> *Do you really think that?*
> *Do you go along with that?*
> *Wouldn't you say that . . . ?*
> *Surely you don't think that . . . ?*
>
> ---
>
> See also *Finding out if everyone agrees* on page 21.

Groupwork

Decide which of the following explanations for what happened in the pictures on pages 52 and 53 is the most likely. Take it in turns to ask the other students whether they agree with each statement or not. Use the expressions on the Function File card.

1 There's been an earthquake.
2 There's been an accident.
3 It's a publicity stunt.
4 There's been an explosion.
5 There's been a fire.
6 It's due to sabotage.

3.2 🎧 Interpreting attitudes

Listen to some people talking about the hotel in the picture on page 52. As you listen, decide how they feel about what has happened. Which words best sum up the attitude of the speakers?

1 _____
2 _____
3 _____
4 _____
5 _____

A upset
B angry
C excited
D not sorry
E puzzled
F guilty
G relieved
H bored

Yesterday and today • **Module 3B**

4.0 🎤 **Commenting on what you see**

Loft extension

Look at the advertisement and individually make notes to prepare a one-minute description of the Smiths' house (the one on the left) and the attitudes and problems of the people living in it.

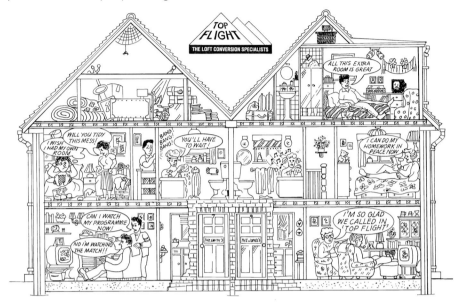

Take it in turns to describe the house and the Smiths to a partner. Use the minute to include everything you prepared in your notes and do not waste time talking about something off the point. Your partner will time you and stop you, if necessary, after one minute.

Exam hint

Remember what is being tested in Part 2 is not just your ability to keep talking, but your ability to talk about what the examiner asks you to talk about. If you simply describe the picture and do not mention the attitudes and problems of those living there, you have failed to take up the opportunity to show what you can do.

4.1 🎤 **Comparing and contrasting**

> COMPARING
>
> Which two expressions mean 'generally speaking'?
> Which expression sounds rather rude and dismissive?
> Can you add any other expressions to the list?
>
> ―――――――――――――――――――――――
>
> *If you compare . . .*
> *On the whole . . .*
> *You just can't compare . . .*
> *I just don't see how you can compare . . .*
> *Come off it! There's no comparison between . . .*
> *By and large . . .*

Pairwork

Discuss with a partner how the loft extension in the Jones's house has changed the appearance of the building and the quality of life of the people living in it. Use the expressions on the Function File card.
How effective is the advert in persuading people to invest in a loft extension? Would you be persuaded by it? Why?

Module 3B • Speaking

4.2 🎤 Explaining how you feel

> **EXPLAINING HOW YOU FEEL ABOUT SOMETHING**
>
> Which expressions are often used before making a personal 'confession'?
> Can you add any other expressions to the list?
>
> *Well, the thing is . . .*
> *The reason is that . . .*
> *Let me explain . . . you see . . .*
> *That's because . . .*
> *The fact is . . .*
> *To be honest . . .*

Personal experience

Take one minute to tell a partner what you feel about where you live at the moment. Explain what you enjoy or sometimes find slightly annoying about living there and give your reasons. Use the expressions on the Function File card. Your partner will stop you after one minute.

🎤 Exam practice

Urban sprawl

Student A
Look at the three drawings showing how one area of the countryside has changed over many years and describe to a partner what has happened and how the lives of the people living in this area have been affected by the development. Say whether you think the changes have been for the better or for the worse.

Student B
Listen to your partner's description and when they have finished, say whether you agree with their opinion.

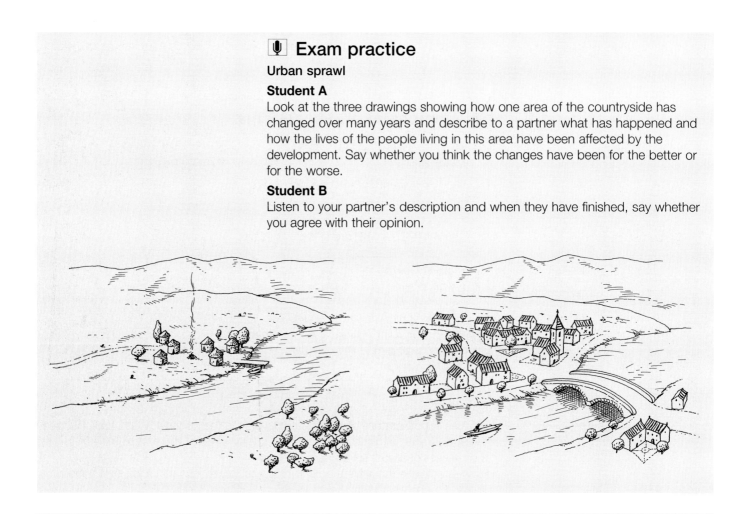

Yesterday and today • Module **3B**

Farming – then and now

Student B

Look at the three drawings showing how a small farm has changed over the years and describe to a partner what has happened to it and how the lives of the people living in it have been affected by the changes. Say whether you think the changes have been for the better or for the worse.

Student A

Listen to your partner's description and when they have finished, say whether you agree with their opinion.

There are more Paper 5 Part 2 tasks in the Task bank on pages 88–91.

3C/D Art and culture

Spotlight on Paper 5 Parts 3 and 4

1.0 🎤 **Collaborating and summing up**

> **SUMMING UP**
>
> Which expression implies two possibilities?
> Which expression might be used after rather a lengthy discussion?
>
> ---
>
> *Basically, it's a question of whether ...*
> *In brief, ...*
> *In a word, ...*
> *So, what we're saying is ...*
> *So, to sum up ...*
> *In other words, ...*

In small groups decide what this picture might be advertising. Use the expressions on the Function File card to summarize what you decided, then tell another group what your decision was.

1.1 🎧 **Saying whether you are interested**

Work through the Function File cards, then listen to what the picture in 1.0 is advertising and say whether you are interested in what you hear or not.

> **SAYING YOU ARE INTERESTED**
>
> Which expression suggests that you are 'crazy' about something?
> Can you add any expressions to the list?
>
> ---
>
> *I'm very keen on ...*
> *I find ... fascinating.*
> *Actually, this type of ... really interests me.*
> *I'm a bit of a fanatic.*

Art and culture • Module 3C/D

SAYING YOU AREN'T INTERESTED

Which expression is very informal?
Which is rather abrupt and rude?
Can you add any other expressions to the list?

I find … rather boring.
… isn't my kind of thing at all.
I can't say I have any great interest in …
I couldn't care less about …

2.0 🎤 Saying something is (in)appropriate

A Choose two pictures and describe them to a partner so that they can identify them.

B Decide together which men's and women's clothes illustrated above you think would be suitable for the occasions listed below, and say why, using the expressions on the Function File card. You may have some ideas of your own for suitable occasions for the clothes!

a picnic outdoors   a fancy dress party   a hiking trip   city sightseeing
a formal dinner   a wedding   working in an office

SAYING SOMETHING IS (IN)APPROPRIATE

Which expression sounds very informal and rather dismissive?
Which expressions would **you** use?
Can you add any other expressions?

I think this would be appropriate for …
If you were going to …, you might / could / should wear …
This looks too formal / informal for …
I wouldn't be seen dead in …
This would(n't) be suitable for …
This would be highly inappropriate for …

Module 3C/D • Speaking

2.1 🎤 Saying something is or isn't fashionable

In small groups, discuss what is or isn't fashionable at the moment in your country, e.g. clothes, hairstyles, jewellery, shoes, then say whether you like or dislike the current fashions. Use expressions from the Function File card.

SAYING SOMETHING IS OR ISN'T FASHIONABLE

Which expression suggests that something is horribly old-fashioned?
Which expression suggests that something is extremely popular?
Which expressions are very informal?

... is / are all the rage at the moment!
... went out with the ark!
... is / are 'in' this summer.
... is / are unpopular / unfashionable.
It's trendy to wear ...
... are really trendy.

3.0 🎤 Making a choice

Work through the Function File card then do the groupwork activities A and B.

MAKING A CHOICE

Which would not impress the examiner, although it is a perfectly valid comment to make? Why not?
Can you add any other expressions to the list?

I definitely wouldn't select this one because ...
Although this one seems ..., it wouldn't ...
Just glancing at them quickly I'd go for ...
This one's certainly a possibility because ...
This certainly wouldn't be my choice because ...
Definitely this one.

National monument (Groupwork)
A Funds are available to build a new national monument in your country to commemorate a special occasion. Look at this list of suggested commemorations and decide what to commemorate.

- a famous writer or artist
- a religious leader
- a great politician
- a national event which changed history
- a great achievement
- an important birth or wedding
- an invention or discovery
- the end of an era

B Various suggestions for what kind of monument it should be have been put forward. Decide what kind of monument you would like to erect and where you would erect it. You can use the designs and suggestions below to help you or you can suggest something different.

Module 3C/D • Speaking

3.1 🎤 Arguing for and against

Divide into groups of four to six. Half of each group will be Team A, and the other half Team B.

You are going to argue about this statement.

Team A

You agree with the statement. Each member of the team must speak for 30 seconds, and should prepare to put forward a different argument in favour of the statement to Team B. First, look at the Function File card together.

ARGUING FOR

Which expression suggests you are approving someone else's proposal?
Which expression conveys less than enthusiastic support?

I can't see anything against . . .
I'm all for / in favour of . . .
I'd certainly give . . . my support.
It would make sense to . . .
There's a lot to be said for . . .

Allow yourselves two or three minutes to prepare what you are going to say. These ideas might help you:

- culture for all
- money available
- educational
- importance of our heritage

Art and culture • Module 3C/D

Team B

You disagree with the statement. Each member of the team must speak for 30 seconds, and should prepare to put forward a different argument against the statement to Team A. First, look at the Function File card together.

ARGUING AGAINST

Which expression sounds very informal?
Which expression sounds rather formal?
Can you add any other expressions to the list?

That's all very well ... but ...
You can't possibly say that ...
It's absolute nonsense to say that ...
I'm dead against ...
I really couldn't condone ...

Allow yourselves two or three minutes to prepare what you are going to say. These ideas might help you:

- who will pay?
- fees minimal
- museums in financial difficulties
- concessions available for students and senior citizens

When everyone is ready, Team A should argue their case, then Team B can reply with theirs. No one should interrupt while someone is speaking!

Which group stated its case most convincingly?

Exam hint

If you can't think of anything to say, relate the statement to the situation in your own country and say whether it works or not!

Now repeat the procedure with Team B agreeing with and Team A disagreeing with this statement.

> **ALL WORKS of ART SHOULD BE RETURNED to the GOVERNMENT of the COUNTRY THEY CAME FROM**

Team B, agree with the statement. These ideas might help you:

- art is part of national heritage
- works of art lose their impact outside their original environment
- only state can afford proper protection
- culture belongs to the people, not just the wealthy

Team A, disagree with the statement. These ideas might help you:

- no funds available to re-purchase
- corrupt state could misuse privilege
- owners not prepared to sell
- suggestion undemocratic

Which group stated its case most convincingly?

4.0 🎤 Collaborating and reporting

Spot the forgery

Look at the two pictures of Van Gogh's *Dr Paul Gachet* and decide what the differences between them are and which you think is the genuine work of art. Only one is genuine, the other is a forgery!

Report your decisions to another group. Did you agree? You can find the right answer on page 150!

4.1 🎧 Listening for statements the speakers make

A You will hear a news item on the radio in which a reporter and a police commissaire are discussing an art scandal. During the discussion they make various comments. For questions 1 to 12, indicate which comments are made by the reporter and which are made by the Commissaire, by writing

    R (for the reporter)
    C (for the Commissaire)
or N (for neither).

1. Mr and Mrs Van Den Bergen lived rather grandly in the French countryside.
2. The Commissaire doubts whether the loot is recoverable.
3. There hasn't been an art scandal like this for two decades.
4. The forgeries are not on show for the press to see.
5. The pictures will be auctioned.
6. Some of the pictures are worth a lot of money.

Art and culture • Module 3C/D

7 Van Den Bergen sold many of the forgeries in Germany.
8 Police arrested him at home.
9 Local people saw little of Mr Van Den Bergen.
10 Van Den Bergen will spend at least three years in prison.
11 Art collectors can now breathe a sigh of relief!
12 Van Den Bergen might not be allowed to paint in prison.

B Analyse your success or failure. Look at the tapescript on page 135 and compare the script with the reformulated statements. What helped you to recognize the statements the speakers made?

4.2 Arguing for and against

Optional speaking activity (Groupwork)

In groups of four or five argue for and against the following statement.

> It makes no difference if a work of art is a forgery – it's still a work of art!

You can refer back to the Function File cards in 3.1 if you wish. You may interrupt each other but do so politely!

Exam hint

Even if you personally don't like any of the alternatives provided, look for something which attracts or interests you slightly about one of them. In this way you can give the examiner a wider sample of language for assessment.

Exam practice

Art scholarship (Groupwork)

Look at the pictures of sculptures by local artists. Talk about what the artists might be trying to express in their work, then decide which sculptor should win a scholarship worth $30,000 to go and study anywhere in the world for a year.

Take three or four minutes to discuss and decide.
Now discuss these questions.

1 What makes a work of art famous or expensive?
2 Why do people collect works of art?
3 Why is an artist's life often a very difficult one?
4 How can we help young artists to realize their potential?

There are more Paper 5 Parts 3 and 4 tasks in the Task bank on pages 91–95.

4 LISTENING

A Achievements

B Survival

C A question of gender

D Points of view

4A Achievements

Spotlight on Paper 4 Part 1

1.0 🎧 **Justifying selection**

You will hear four people talking about inventions. Write down what they consider to be the 'greatest little invention'.

Great little inventions

1 _____

2 _____

3 _____

4 _____

Which of these 'little inventions' do you consider to be the greatest and why? What other 'great little inventions' would you add to the list?

1.1 🎧 **Listening for more precise information**

You will hear a talk about an inventor. Read through the notes below then, as you listen, fill in the missing information.

A bright spark: Joseph Wilson Swan

Born: (1)_____

Died: (2)_____

Aged 13 started work as (3)_____

1846 qualified as a (4)_____

Company also manufactured (5)_____

1862 patented a method of (6)_____

1862 married (7)_____

1871 married (8)_____

Exam hint

Don't waste time agonizing over spelling! Write your answer in pencil quickly, check it on the second listening, then make your final decision about spelling as you transfer your answers to the answer sheet, or the OMR (Optical Mark Reader) as it is called.

Number of children: (9) _____

Began to study (10) _____

1879 in public presented the (11) _____

1881 formed a company called The (12) _____

1883 Swan formed a partnership with (13) _____

In his lifetime he received many (14) _____

1.2 🎤 Interpreting in more depth what you hear

Exam hint

Understanding the implications of what you hear, rather than just listening to the words spoken, will help you to take in what is being said and to focus on the information you need to listen for to complete the tasks in the exam.

Pairwork

Discuss answers to the following questions about the talk in 1.1. You may need to listen to the tape again, but not all the information needed to answer the questions appears *explicitly* on the tape and there may be more than one possible answer.

1. Where do you think he might have met his first wife?
2. Why do you think he eventually married her sister? (several possible answers here!)
3. Why was the audience in Newcastle 'fascinated'?
4. How did Swan help Edison?
5. Why is Edison's name more well-known than Swan's?
6. What kind of recognition, besides a knighthood, might Swan have received?

Compare your answers with another pair of students.

2.0 🎧 Listening for missing information

You will hear someone talking about a book award. Read through the following notes then, as you listen, fill in the missing information.

Book award

Title of award: (1) _____

Awarded for books which people (2) _____

To be shortlisted, books must make readers want to (3) _____

Competition judged by people who read only (4) _____

Prizewinner to be announced (5) _____

Can you explain what the title of the award means?

Module 4A • Listening

2.1 🎧 Listening for a storyline

You will hear someone talking about two of the books shortlisted for the prize mentioned in 2.0. Read through the following summaries of the books then, as you listen, fill in the missing information.

A simple plan

While trying to escape from a (1)_____, three men find a plane which (2)_____, a pilot who is (3)_____ and (4)_____ in a bag. They decide to (5)_____ but the scheme results in one of the characters being (6)_____.
The book has been described as an original (7)_____.

Night shall overtake us

Four schoolgirls swear that they will always (8)_____. They will soon face the horror of the (9)_____, in which their lives will be turned (10)_____. Aurora first campaigns for the right to (11)_____ and then becomes (12)_____.
It's a saga of tragedy, unrestrained passion and (13)_____. The reader is constantly wondering who will be the first to (14)_____.

2.2 🎤 Making a choice

Which novel in 2.1 would you prefer to read? Which do you think might win the prize? Give reasons for your answer.

3.0 🎤 Coping with fame

What would be the positive and negative aspects of being well-known or famous? How would you feel if you were well-known or famous?

3.1 🎧 Predicting quickly what something is about

A You will hear someone being interviewed. Before listening to the interview, read through the following questions.

1. Who is going to be interviewed?
2. What was his previous job?
3. What is he about to become?
4. What is he finally described as?

Exam hint

In the exam you can usually predict, to a certain extent, what you are going to hear by reading through the task questions carefully. This will make you more confident about the listening task and help you to focus on the answers to the task questions.

Achievements • **Module 4A**

B Now, as you listen to the interview, make brief notes to help you answer the questions.

3.2 🎧 Listening for statements the speakers make

Exam hint

Remember, the statements made will not repeat word for word what the speakers say on the tape. You should be looking for the information on the tape expressed in a different way. In addition, the comments the speakers do not make might look plausible as you read through them. You will have to listen very carefully to decide whether they were actually made or not.

Read through the statements below then listen to the rest of the programme mentioned in 3.1. During the interview various comments are made. Indicate which comments are being made by Sam and which by the interviewer by writing
  S (for Sam)
  I (for the interviewer)
or N (for neither)

1 Sam's writing career began at university.
2 Getting the novel accepted for publication was not a problem.
3 Sam enjoyed his modelling assignments in Europe.
4 Sam's modelling success was immediate.
5 Sam could have carried on being a model.
6 Sam's written a story about the future.
7 The modelling world has many advantages.
8 Sam has friends in high places.
9 Sam's future looks bright.

3.3 🎧 Recognizing words in context

Often the words you hear on tape are confusing. You might mistakenly hear the wrong word (*hair* instead of *hare*), the wrong pronunciation (*dim* instead of *din*), or the wrong stress and pronunciation (**harm**ful instead of **half full**). However, the context will usually help you to identify most of the words you hear.

You will hear ten shorter comments similar to those you heard in the interview in 3.2. However, the speakers use one inappropriate word in each comment. Write down the inappropriate word, then try to supply the appropriate one.

1 _____ _____   6 _____ _____
2 _____ _____   7 _____ _____
3 _____ _____   8 _____ _____
4 _____ _____   9 _____ _____
5 _____ _____   10 _____ _____

4.0 🎧 Understanding and remembering longer pieces of information

Listen to the introduction to a radio programme called *The Power of The Press*. As you listen, make a note of the question the lady in the Midlands asks. You may need to listen twice.

Before you hear the results of the investigation, what do you think the answer is going to be?

Module 4A • Listening

4.1 🎧 Following a line of development

Exam hint
It is useful to be able to match information you hear on tape with similar information in the task questions. This will help you follow the line of development in the listening extract and identify statements speakers make.

You will hear the rest of Peter Rainer's report. The following points were all made but they are in the wrong order. Read through the points carefully, then, as you listen, arrange them in their order of appearance on the tape. Write the numbers 1–8 beside the points as they are mentioned. The first three are done for you.

A *The Times* received more correspondence about poor children than it had about any other issue.
B Reports of the death of a young boy in care appeared in the newspapers.
C Social Services departments were set up.
D Lady Allen made the public aware of the unsatisfactory arrangements made for children in care. *1*
E Children's departments came into being.
F Lady Allen pointed out that society 'looked down on' needy children. *2*
G The government set up a committee to investigate the plight of orphaned children.
H Lady Allen demanded a public enquiry. *3*

Compare your answers with those of another student.

4.2 🎤 Discussing

Groupwork

Discuss the following questions. Allow four or five minutes, then compare your decisions with those of another group.

1 What are the differences between a tabloid newspaper, the 'gutter' press and a quality newspaper?
2 Why do newspapers usually contain more 'bad' than 'good' news items?
3 How far do you think newspapers influence what people think?

Exam practice: gap-fill

You will hear a radio presenter and an airline employee talking about language courses for the cabin staff of an airline company. For questions 1–10 complete the missing information with an appropriate word or short phrase. You will hear the recording twice.

Crew are not taught the (1)_____ used in some grammar books.

Instructors use (2)_____ to teach the crew foreign languages.

Lessons might take place in a (3)_____ of part of an aircraft or a restaurant (4)_____.

Today the airline employs more (5)_____ than it did previously.

The language trainers are extremely (6)_____.

Bill Brown became (7)_____ six years ago.

Language classes are targeted mainly at (8)_____ crew.

Provision is also made for (9)_____ crew.

On a special (10)_____ crew can try out one of the courses.

There are more Paper 4 Part 1 tasks in the Task bank on pages 96–98.

4B Survival

Spotlight on Paper 4 Part 2

1.0 🎤 **Interpreting artwork**

Pairwork

Decide what point the picture might be making and whether it is making it successfully. Compare your decisions with those of another pair of students.

1.1 🎧 **Relating what you see to what you hear**

You will hear three speakers talking about the environment. They all make at least two of the points A to I. Read through the points then, as you listen, decide which points each speaker makes. No point is made twice and one point is not made at all. Listen only once.

Speaker 1	Speaker 2	Speaker 3
1 _____	4 _____	7 _____
2 _____	5 _____	8 _____
3 _____	6 _____	

Points made
A Other things more important than the environment
B Cut consumption of natural resources
C Government lacking in policies
D Attitudes of those involved unsympathetic
E Problem a sensitive one
F Not much time left
G No action to date
H New projects should be environment-friendly
I Future success relies on solar power

1.2 🎤 **Evaluating the opinions of others**

Groupwork

Decide which speaker you identify with most. Report back to another group giving reasons for your opinions.

Module 4B • Listening

2.0

> **Exam hint**
> Don't be tempted to answer questions using prior knowledge or by guessing only. The answer must match the information on the tape – it might be what you think or it might be something completely different!

🎧 Identifying information which is repeated in some way

You will hear a radio programme about different ways to beat stress. Read through the notes then, as you listen, fill in the missing information. You will hear the recording only once.

Stressbusters

Aerobic exercise usually makes you (1)_____.

The Alexander Technique is very useful when (2)_____ symptoms are connected.

Relaxation tapes are often prescribed for very (3)_____.

Don't be put off yoga by the thought of (4)_____.

2.1

> **Exam hint**
> As you read through a list of options, identify the key words and try to match them to what you hear on the tape.

🎧 Identifying pros (arguments for) and cons (arguments against)

A Read through the list of pros relating to the Stressbusters, then, as you listen, match the points you hear to the four different ways of 'busting' stress. One point is not made. You will hear the recording only once.

Aerobic exercise
1 _____
2 _____

Alexander Technique
3 _____
4 _____

Relaxation tapes
5 _____
6 _____

Yoga
7 _____
8 _____

Pros
A helps back and shoulder problems
B no age limits
C easy to organize
D no special equipment needed
E meets your special needs
F keeps you fit
G you don't have to be 'good at it'
H cheap
I you make friends

B Now read through the list of cons. Then, as you listen, match the points made to the four different ways of 'busting' stress. Again, one point is not needed. You will hear the recording only once.

Aerobic exercise
1 _____
2 _____

Alexander Technique
3 _____
4 _____

Relaxation tapes
5 _____
6 _____

Yoga
7 _____
8 _____

Cons
A does not benefit young people
B needs a series of lessons
C involves a lot of effort
D can be boring
E high risk of injury
F not active enough
G family make fun of you
H often difficult to fit into your routine
I no immediate benefits

2.2 🎧 Spelling words you hear

Listen to ten words which appeared on the tape in 2.0 and 2.1 and see if you can spell them correctly.

1 _____   6 _____
2 _____   7 _____
3 _____   8 _____
4 _____   9 _____
5 _____   10 _____

Check your spellings then use the words in a sentence of your own to show that you understand their meaning.

3.0 🎧 Identifying information which is recycled in some way

You will hear someone talking about North American mountain lions. Read through the notes, then, as you listen, complete the missing information. You will hear the recording only once.

Earthwatch and the North American mountain lions

If you come into close contact with a North American mountain lion, you should (1)_____.

US game agencies know (2)_____ the lion.

Earthwatch started (3)_____ in 1972.

One aim of *Earthwatch* is to understand what affects the (4)_____ on earth.

Earthwatch is a welcome change from (5)_____.

Earthwatch will take you to the (6)_____.

To join the party, you need to be (7)_____.

3.1 🎤 Identifying what you hear

The left-hand words all appeared on the tape in 3.0. Read them aloud together with the right-hand words and mark the strong and weak stresses. Not all the words are stressed differently!

1	persecuted	persecution	7 familiar	familiarity
2	human	humanity	8 commercial	commerce
3	direct (adj)	direct (verb)	9 company	companion
4	organized	organization	10 accommodation	accommodate
5	projects (noun)	projects (verb)	11 real	reality
6	scientific	scientist	12 information	inform

Now use one of the words from each pair in a sentence of your own.

Module 4B • Listening

3.2 🎤 Discussing

Groupwork

Decide what the positive and negative aspects of a holiday with *Earthwatch* might be and whether you would like to go on this type of holiday or not.

4.0 🎧 Identifying information which is recycled in some way

Re-enacting a battle scene

Listen to an announcer speaking at an open-air re-enactment of a battle and decide whether the following statements are made by the announcer. Write either Y (for yes) or N (for no) next to each statement. Listen only once.

1. The Society is commemorating a battle which took place between fellow countrymen.
2. The exact site of the battle is unknown.
3. The battle decided what kind of government the country was to have.
4. This is one of the most ambitious of the Society's re-enactments.
5. There are other entertainments available at this event.
6. The crowd are all wearing costumes of the period.
7. Some of those involved in the fighting are women.
8. Spectators seem to be bunched together in one area.

4.1 🎤 Describing a re-enactment

Pairwork

Student A

Look at the photograph from a programme for the Sealed Knot Society on page 113 and describe the scene which is being re-enacted. You have one minute to do this. Do not show your picture to your partner.

Student B

Look at the photograph on page 124. It is similar to the one your partner is going to describe. As you listen to your partner describing their photograph, see if you can find two things which are the same and two things which are different in your picture. When your partner has finished, talk about the similarities and differences.

4.2 🎤 Saying you'd rather not / you aren't sure / you'd like to

Simulation (Groupwork)

Student A

You are about to become a member of the Sealed Knot Society but your friends are not very enthusiastic about joining. Try to persuade them to join. You could mention these points.

- the excitement
- travel
- raising money for charity
- making friends
- learning about history

Other students

You have been invited by Student A to become a member of the Sealed Knot Society. Using the expressions on the Function File cards, say whether you'd like to or not and give your reasons.

SAYING YOU'D RATHER NOT

Which sentences express the most reluctance?
Which sentence offers an excuse?
Add expressions of your own to the list.

Well, I'd rather not, if you don't mind.
I don't really feel it's my kind of thing.
You can count me out!
It seems a strange sort of thing to do, if you ask me.
Actually, I don't really think I could find the time.

SAYING YOU AREN'T SURE

Which expressions suggest that the speaker might never get round to making a decision?
Can you add any expressions of your own?

Hmm . . . I'd have to think about it.
Well, I'm in two minds about it really.
I can't make up my mind.
I'm not altogether sure I'd enjoy it.

SAYING YOU'D LIKE TO

Which sentence sounds too enthusiastic?
Which sounds as if the speaker is slightly less keen on the idea?
Can you add any other expressions?

That sounds a great idea.
I think I might be able to work up some enthusiasm for the idea.
Can't think of anything I'd like better.
Never in my wildest dreams did I imagine I'd . . .

Module 4C • Listening

🎧 Exam practice: gap-fill

Listen to a presenter on the radio talking about the Sealed Knot Society and for questions 1–8 complete the sentences. **Listen very carefully as you will hear the recording ONCE only.**

The founder of the Sealed Knot had studied (1)_____ history. One of its

aims is to interest (2)_____ in the civil war. The Sealed Knot has

(3)_____ than any other European Re-enactment Society.

There are, however, no (4)_____ members.

Some of their profits are given to different (5)_____ each year.

The Society is able to attract (6)_____.

The Society is prepared to attend (7)_____ if asked.

The Society conjures up the past to help the (8)_____.

There are more Paper 4 Part 2 tasks in the Task bank on pages 98–100.

4C A question of gender

Spotlight on Paper 4 Part 3

1.0   🎤 **Collaborating**

Female / Male preconceptions
Do you consider that women and girls have different personalities from men and boys? In groups of three list two attributes you feel are more characteristically female, and two male, then compare your lists with another group.

♀(F)   ♂(M)

_____   _____

_____   _____

1.1   🎧 **Listening for specific details**

You will hear a list of five attributes. As you listen, fill in the missing information.

awareness of (1)_____

(2)_____ ability

(3)_____ skills

thinking (4)_____

remembering (5)_____

A question of gender • Module 4C

1.2 🎤 **Expressing personal opinions**

In the same groups as for 1.0, decide which of the attributes in the list in 1.1 you regard as being more characteristically female or male.

_____   _____

_____   _____

_____   _____

2.0 🎤 **Testing preconceptions**

Test the opinions you expressed in 1.0 and 1.2 with these gender-sensitive questions. Allow yourselves about five minutes.

❶ **Which two figures below are identical to the figure in the square?**

      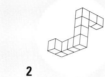

                  1   2   3   4

❷ **Study the objects in group A for one minute and cover it up. Then look at group B and put an X through the figures not in the original array. Score one point for each item correctly crossed out and subtract one point for each item incorrectly crossed out.**

A    B

❸ **Name as many synonyms for the following words as you can in three minutes:**   **clear   dark   strong   wild**

Module 4C • Listening

2.1 🎧 Listening for facts and figures

Listen to the official results of the gender sensitive questions and complete the missing information.

1

Numbers (a) _____ same

(b) _____% of women and (c) _____% of men scored correctly.

2

The perfect score: (d) _____

Average score for women: (e) _____

Average score for men: (f) _____

3

Average score for women: (g) _____ per word

Average score for men: (h) _____ per word

What is your reaction to the results? Are you surprised / interested / sceptical / reassured? Explain why.

2.2 🎧 Evaluating preconceptions and selecting

Female versus male

You will hear seven statements on tape. Listen to them carefully, and write down three of them which might be based on the results of the gender-sensitive questions in 2.0.

1 _____

2 _____

3 _____

Compare your choices with the rest of the class.

3.0 🎤 Trying to decipher notes

The following notes were made while listening to two statements about perception. Can you reconstruct them so that they make sense?

Statement 1
M better at think 3 dimens. Poss. ∵ hunting. req. orient. when look. prey.

Statement 2
F better at rememb. locat. Poss. ∵ forag. food. When look food must rememb. unconnec. items.

3.1 🎧 Comparing notes

Cover the notes you read in 3.0. You will hear the two statements which were made about perception. Listen to them twice, and, as you listen, take notes. When you have finished, compare your notes with those you tried to decipher in 3.0.

A question of gender • Module 4C

> **Exam hint**
> You may not understand the precise meaning of a word or know how to spell it, but may know what it means in context. Use the word you know (*remember* instead of *recall*) if it conveys what you want to say.

Statement 1 _____

Statement 2 _____

Now, without looking at your notes or statements, try to express in your own words what the speakers are saying.

3.2 🎤 Expressing personal opinions

In small groups, decide whether you think there is any truth in the statements in 3.1. Be ready to give reasons for your opinions.

4.0 🎧 Identifying comments the speakers make

You will hear a scientist and a radio reporter on an educational programme talking about male and female differences in animal species. During the interview they make various comments. For questions 1–16 indicate which comments are being expressed by Sally, the scientist, and which are expressed by Martin, the reporter, by writing

   S (for Sally)
   M (for Martin)
or N (for neither).

You will hear the recording twice.

> **Exam hint**
> You may know something about the subject, but you must indicate only the comments the speakers make.

turtle

whiptail lizard

jacana bird

cichlid

1 We humans expect the animal world to behave as we do.
2 Turtle eggs are laid in the sand.
3 Only female turtles are hatched in sunny places.
4 After hatching, male and female turtles seek shady places.
5 There are no male whiptail lizards.
6 Fertilization of the lizards' eggs takes place just before hatching.
7 Whiptails are related to prehistoric creatures.
8 Whiptails retain some of the habits of their ancestors.
9 Female jacana birds eat more food than males.
10 Male jacanas build the nests.
11 Jacana eggs take a long time to hatch.
12 Female jacanas often have more than one partner.
13 There are three different sexes in the cichlid species.
14 The female cichlid is less brightly coloured than the male.
15 Most people learn about these fish at school.
16 Some of these fish can change their colour.

Module 4C • Listening

5.0

Exam hint

Correct spelling is important in Paper 4 but you will not lose marks for spelling a proper noun incorrectly if it is an acceptable variation, e.g. *Hurst*, *Hearst*, *Hirst*.

🎧 Matching sounds to spellings

You will hear 14 words read out on tape. (These words will appear later in the exam practice.) As you listen, write down the words you hear. The last two words are people's names!

1 _____   6 _____   11 _____

2 _____   7 _____   12 _____

3 _____   8 _____   13 _____

4 _____   9 _____   14 _____

5 _____   10 _____

Compare your list of words with a partner's. If they do not match, e.g. genes / jeans / Jean's, check in the tapescript on page 138 to see if you have the correct spellings of the words, then find out what the words mean.

🎧 Exam practice: identifying comments

You will hear part of a discussion on a radio programme in which two teachers, Mary and David, are discussing making sense of the differences between women and men.

During the discussion they make various comments. For questions 1 to 9, indicate which comments are being expressed by Mary and which by David by writing

   M (for Mary)
   D (for David)
or N (for neither)

You will hear the recording twice.

1 Teachers expect boys to make a greater contribution than girls in class.
2 Girls are better at expressing their opinions in a classroom situation.
3 Girls do better in maths when there are no boys present.
4 It seems that there is no fundamental difference between male and female brains.
5 A real difference between male and female abilities poses problems for the educationalists.
6 Americans have taken male / female differences into account in their primary school curriculum.
7 I did some research into male and female roles in different countries.
8 Studies which prove that there are no male / female differences rarely make the headlines.
9 The answer to our problems lies in our genetic make-up.

There are more Paper 4 Part 3 tasks in the Task bank on pages 100–104.

4D Points of view

Spotlight on Paper 4 Part 4

1.0 🎧 Identifying attitudes

You will hear three speakers. Decide which is expressing the attitudes below.

	Disbelief	Boredom	Pleasure
Speaker 1			
Speaker 2			
Speaker 3			

What helped you to make your decision?

1.1 🎧 Recognizing degrees of certainty

You will hear six statements. Decide which speakers sound fairly certain and which sound less certain.

	Fairly certain	Less certain
Speaker 1		
Speaker 2		
Speaker 3		
Speaker 4		
Speaker 5		
Speaker 6		

What helped you to decide?

1.2 🎤 Checking to make sure you are right

Pairwork

Take it in turns to ask your partner questions 1 to 10, using question tags. Express your certainty or uncertainty by using either a falling or a rising intonation in the question tag and see if your partner can recognize which you are expressing.

You want to check that:

1 your partner has seen a recent film.
2 the post has arrived.
3 the weather forecast for today was good.
4 the manager left a message.
5 inflation will come down.
6 your partner wants to come to the dance.
7 your partner agrees with you.
8 the journey will take about three hours.
9 Brazil won the World Cup in 1994.
10 vegans eat meat.

Module 4D • Listening

2.0 🎧 Listening for different points of view

You will hear five different people talking on a TV 'phone-in' about TV programmes broadcast on that channel. As you listen decide what type of programme the speakers are talking about, what their reaction to it was and why they reacted in this way. Some of the information has been filled in already. You may need to listen twice.

	Type of programme	Reaction	Reasons for reaction
Speaker 1	a series on sport	(1)	(2)
Speaker 2	(3)	delighted / fascinated by the subject	(4)
Speaker 3	(5)	(6)	wrong place, awful weather, not tempted by the food
Speaker 4	(7)	not amused / angry	(8)
Speaker 5	the weather forecast	(9)	(10)

2.1 🎤 Recalling what points the speakers made

The following expressions were used by the five different speakers in 2.0. Can you remember what points they were making? Try to complete the sentences using words and expressions of your own. (They may be different from what you heard on the tape.)
When you have finished, listen again and check your answers.

Speaker 1
As if we didn't have enough . . . !
Isn't it about time TV channels . . . ?

Speaker 2
May I congratulate you on . . . ?
Many thanks for what I consider to be . . . !

Speaker 3
I just had to ring and say . . . !
It's not my idea of fun . . . !

Speaker 4
How you can possibly call . . . beats me.
For one thing, . . .
and for another . . . !

Speaker 5
Is there any chance of us . . . ?
You'd think that with all this . . . they'd be . . .

3.0 🎧 Identifying the points the speaker is making

Before you listen to the tape, read through the multiple choice questions.

Speaker 1

1 According to the first speaker, last night the west of the country suffered
   A scattered showers.
   B gale force winds.
   C severe flooding.

2 He wants to
   A encourage people to help others in difficulties.
   B warn people of worse conditions to come.
   C request help from the emergency services.

Speaker 2

3 The second speaker is hoping to
   A recruit senior management consultants.
   B advertise courses in human resources.
   C raise money to finance business courses.

4 She invites anyone who might be interested to
   A visit her.
   B write to her.
   C phone her.

Speaker 3

5 The third speaker is suggesting that certain characters in classical mythology
   A were all-powerful in their time.
   B have little relevance nowadays.
   C were experts at navigation.

6 She also suggests that if you are thinking of seeing the new opera at the Classic Theatre,
   A you would be better off staying at home.
   B you should book now to avoid disappointment.
   C you should listen to the CD first.

Speaker 4

7 The fourth speaker is suggesting ways of
   A helping people to bring up children.
   B occupying the children when they're not at school.
   C finding a hobby which will help you to relax.

8 But she warns anyone thinking of taking this up that
   A adults need a licence.
   B you need to be a member of a club.
   C it won't appeal to teenagers.

Speaker 5

9 The fifth speaker says that the late Geoff McQueen
   A began his career writing plays for TV.
   B wrote about people he knew personally.
   C had travelled all over the world.

10 He advises everyone
    A not to miss McQueen reruns on TV.
    B to go and see a McQueen play at the theatre.
    C to read one of McQueen's plays.

You will hear five different speakers on the radio. As you listen, choose the correct option **A**, **B** or **C**.

Module 4D • Listening

3.1 🎤 **Thinking of similar sounds (homophones)**

These words all appeared on the tape in 3.0. Try to think of another word with the same pronunciation but a different spelling and meaning for each one.

1	night	_____	7 so	_____
2	days	_____	8 made	_____
3	great	_____	9 rights	_____
4	role	_____	10 new	_____
5	for	_____	11 died	_____
6	hours	_____	12 seen	_____

4.0 🎧 **Identifying speakers**

Exam hint

Remember that in the exam you will have to choose five out of eight options (A to H).

You will hear various people speaking about different topics. Listen to the tape once and match the extracts 1–5 with the people.

A a married person
B a politician
C a scientist
D a teacher
E a mother
F an astronaut
G a student
H a customer
I a doctor

1	
2	
3	
4	
5	

4.1 🎧 **Identifying the points the speakers are making**

Listen again to the same people and match the extracts with the points the speakers are making. Remember, you only need to choose five!

A suggesting a remedy
B apportioning blame
C assessing the effects of a personal habit
D listing the benefits
E suggesting a reason for a fall in standards
F emphasizing the importance of competition
G expressing reservations about who takes responsibility
H giving an order
I criticizing the older generation

1	
2	
3	
4	
5	

4.2 🎧 Making a logical guess about spelling

Listen to 12 words which appeared on the tape in 4.0 and 4.1 and see if you can spell them correctly.

1 _____   7 _____
2 _____   8 _____
3 _____   9 _____
4 _____   10 _____
5 _____   11 _____
6 _____   12 _____

Which spelling rules do they conform to, if any? You may want to look back to the spelling rules on pages 9 and 26.

🎧 Exam practice: multiple matching

You will hear various people talking about life. You will hear the recording twice.

Task one
For questions 1–5, match the extracts as you hear them with the people A–H.

A car mechanic
B computer operator
C taxi driver
D cleaner
E cashier
F train driver
G police officer
H TV repairer

	1
	2
	3
	4
	5

Task two
For questions 6–10, match the extracts as you hear them with the attitudes towards life A–H.

A accepts responsibility
B takes life seriously
C looks on the bright side
D couldn't care less
E thinks it's great to be alive
F gets depressed
G is a 'loner'
H thinks life's all a joke

	6
	7
	8
	9
	10

There are more Paper 4 Part 4 tasks in the Task bank on pages 104–107.

SPEAKING
Paper 5 Task bank

Activities for Paper 5 Part 1

Make notes as you hear relevant information in these Part 1 tasks. This will help you in the note-taking part of the listening paper.

1 🎤 School days

Finding out about personal experience (Pairwork)

Find out the following information about your partner.

- what kind of nursery / primary / secondary school they went / go to
- what kind of memories they have of primary or secondary school and why
- how relevant what they learned at school was to what they are doing today
- how they feel the time at school could have been improved

Now tell the class the most interesting piece of information about your partner.

2 🎤 Simulation

Job application (Pairwork)

Student A

You are interested in working abroad and have heard about a vacancy for an English Language Adviser in another country but employed by a university in Wales. Phone the personnel officer at the Welsh university and find out:

- where the job is based.
- what salary is offered.
- what the job involves.
- what qualifications you need.
- what experience you need.
- how long the appointment lasts.

When you have finished, you can compare your notes with the actual job advertisement.

Student B

Your instructions are on page 108.

3 🎤 Simulation

Insurance policy (Pairwork)

Student A

You are going on holiday and want to arrange holiday insurance cover but you are worried about the small print in the policy. Find out from the insurance broker exactly what is on offer.

You want to know:
- what type of insurance the policy offers.
- what the premiums are for (a) children under two.
  (b) other children.
  (c) adults.
  (d) a vehicle.
- what the breakdown and recovery premium for a vehicle covers.
- what compensation you would receive for
  (a) medical expenses.
  (b) loss of or damage to luggage.
- whether you are insured if the company goes bankrupt.

When you have finished, you can compare your notes with the original policy.

Student B

Your instructions are on page 109.

4 Simulation

Mail order query (Pairwork)

Student A

You work for a mail order firm selling compact discs (CDs). Talk to an irritated customer who has ordered three free promotional CDs which have not arrived. Be as patient and polite as possible. You need to find out and make a note of:

- the name of the customer.
- the address and postcode of the customer.
- whether the customer signed the order form.
- the reference numbers of the CDs.
- the title of the CDs and the artists' names.
- whether any payment was sent with the order, e.g. cash, cheque.

Student B

Your instructions are on page 110.

5 Simulation

Holiday villa (Pairwork)

Student A

Someone has recommended the Villa Rosa, in the Mediterranean area, as a good place for you to rent for a holiday and has given you the name of the owner. You are interested but before you make a decision, you need to talk to the owner and make a note of the following:

- where the villa is.
- how many people it sleeps.
- what kind of building it is.
- how much it will cost per week in July.
- whether there is a swimming pool.
- what facilities are available in the area.
- whether you will need a car.
- any other information relevant to your needs.

When you have finished, compare your notes with the advert for the villa.

Student B

Your instructions are on page 111.

Task bank 5B • Speaking

6 🎤 Simulation
Leisure activity enquiry (Pairwork)

Student A

You are on holiday with a group of young people. You have heard about a new leisure activity and are interested in going to celebrate someone's birthday. Phone the information desk and find out and make a note of the following:

- what kind of activity it is.
- whether it's safe.
- when it's open.
- whether you can book in advance.
- how much it costs.
- whether they organize birthday parties.
- what age groups it is suitable for.
- how many people it can accommodate.
- how you get there from the railway station.

When you have finished, compare your notes with the actual advert for the activity.

Student B

Your instructions are on page 112.

Activities for Paper 5 Part 2

These activities are meant to take about one minute for the student who does the main task and about 20 seconds for the follow-up comments from the other student. The shared activities, however, will take longer, as each student should have the opportunity to speak for about one minute. All activities can be used again with different partners or by reversing roles.

1 🎤 Describe and match
Possible suspects (Pairwork)

Student A

Look at the photofit pictures on page 114 of people suspected of having been involved in a crime. Unfortunately they have been muddled up. Choose two halves which you think go together then describe them to a partner.

Student B

Look at the same pictures as your partner and see if you can identify which picture your partner is describing.
Reverse roles and repeat the procedure until you have described all the people.

2 🎤 Describe, compare and speculate
Climbing (Pairwork)

Student A

Look at the pictures on page 126. Compare and contrast the climbers and their equipment, saying what you think might motivate people to climb mountains.

Student B

Look at the same set of pictures. When your partner has finished, say which climbers you think had the more difficult task.

Activities for Paper 5 Part 2 • **Task bank 5B**

3 🎤 Describe and hypothesize

Colourful events (Shared activity for three students)

Look at the pictures on page 115. Choose one of the pictures in the set. It is not necessary to hide your picture from your partners. Take a minute each to describe your picture as fully as possible and suggest what the people are doing and what they might be celebrating. Then see if you agree with your partner's interpretations of their pictures and decide which event would interest you most.

4 🎤 Describe and spot the differences

Ball control (Shared activity for two students)

Look at the pictures on page 116 and page 125. Take a minute each and describe your pictures as fully as possible to one another. **Do not let** your partner see your picture.

When you have finished, see if, together, you can find ten differences between the two pictures. This may take considerably longer than a minute!

5 🎤 Describe and evaluate

Modern sculpture (Pairwork)

Student A

Look at the picture of the sculpture on page 116. Describe your picture as fully as possible and say who you think this type of sculpture might appeal to. **Do not let** your partner see your picture.

Student B

Look at the picture on page 125. **Do not let** your partner see your picture. Listen carefully to your partner and find one thing which is the same in both your pictures and one thing which is different and say whether you agree with your partner's opinion about the sculpture.

Now compare pictures and see how accurate you were!

6 🎤 Describe and hypothesize

Outdoor entertainment (Pairwork)

Student A

Look at the picture on page 117. Describe the street scene and the people in it and suggest who they are and what they might be doing there. **Do not let** your partner see your picture.

Student B

Look at the picture on page 126. **Do not let** your partner see your picture. Listen carefully to your partner's description of a similar picture and see if you can spot two things which are different and two things which are the same in your two pictures.

Now compare pictures and see how accurate you were!

7 🎤 Describe and speculate

Building development (Pairwork)

Student A

Look at the pictures on page 118. Describe these three pictures of different stages in a development project and suggest what the building might now be used for.

Task bank 5B • Speaking

Student B
Look at the same pictures as your partner. Say whether you agree with your partner's suggestion about what the building might be used for. Suggest what other type of building could have been built on that particular site.

8 🎤 Select, describe and speculate

Street market (Pairwork)

Student A
Look at the pictures on page 119. Choose one picture from the set of three and describe it as fully as possible to your partner and say what kind of market you think this is and where it might be.

Student B
Look at the same set of pictures as your partner. Listen carefully to what your partner says and decide which picture they are describing and whether you agree about the type and location of the market.

9 🎤 Describe, compare and hypothesize

Kitchens (Pairwork)

Student A
Look at the pictures on page 120. Describe the pictures of the two kitchens and compare what life must have been like and what it is like today for the person working in them.

Student B
Look at the same set of pictures as your partner. Do you agree with what your partner said about the differences in working in the two types of kitchen? Why?

10 🎤 Describe, hypothesize and evaluate

Art forms (Shared activity for three students)

Students A, B and C
Look at the three pictures on page 121. Choose one picture each and take a minute to describe it to your partners. Mention what form of art is on display, why it might have been created and what your personal opinion about it is. **Do not hide** your pictures from one another.

When you have finished say whether you agree with your partners' opinions and decide which picture shows the type of art form you like best.

11 🎤 Describe, speculate and identify

People on the telephone (Pairwork)

Student A
Look at the set of eight pictures of someone talking on the telephone on page 122 and describe three of them to your partner, saying who you think the person might be talking to.

Student B
Look at the set of pictures on page 127. They are the same as your partner's but they are in a different order. Listen carefully to your partner's description then say which three your partner was describing.

What made the task easy or difficult?

Activities for Paper 5 Parts 3/4 • **Task bank 5C/D**

12 Describe, evaluate and identify

China figures (Pairwork)

Student A
Look at the set of seven pictures of china figures on page 123 and describe to your partner three of the figures, saying what might have inspired their maker to 'immortalize' them in china.

Student B
Look at the set of pictures on page 128. They are the same as your partner's but they are in a different order. Listen carefully to your partner's description then say which three your partner was describing.

Activities For Paper 5 Parts 3 and 4

Appoint a different 'secretary' to take the minutes – in other words, make brief notes on your group decisions – for each point discussed in the activities below. Taking minutes is an excellent way to improve your ability to write and listen at the same time. It will help you with the note-taking tasks in Paper 4 but remember, you must be able to decipher your own notes to report back to your fellow students!

When two students are taking part, these activities should take three or four minutes for Part 3, plus another three or four minutes for the Part 4 further discussion. Extra time should be allowed for more students. Some activities will take longer than the time allowed in the exam but in this part of the speaking test you do not need to be so time-conscious as the examiner will stop you if you overrun!

1 Collaborating / Drawing conclusions / Expressing personal preferences

Dangerous working environments (Groupwork for two or three students)

Part 3
In groups of two or three, look at the pictures and decide:
- what qualities you need for these different jobs.
- which you think is the most dangerous.
- which person would earn the most money.
- who would have the greatest job satisfaction.
- which jobs might well disappear in future and what they might be replaced by.

Task bank 5C/D • Speaking

Part 4
How have the roles of male and female changed in the work force over the last decade or so?
What roles will men and women have in the work force in future?
What kinds of jobs give the greatest satisfaction?
What can be done to help people who are unemployed?

2 🎤 Debating

TV should be banned (Groupwork for about five students)

Two of you should argue the case **for** and two **against** the motion 'TV should be banned'. One student acts as chairperson. Allow yourselves one minute each to express your arguments either for or against the motion. The chairperson will decide who puts forward the most convincing arguments and report back to the rest of the class.

These ideas might help you.

Arguments against
- addictive
- programmes too predictable
- many programmes are rubbish
- bad for the health
- causes arguments about who watches what
- kills conversation
- advertising indoctrinates
- many programmes unsuitable for those who watch them

Arguments for
- useful as background noise
- variety of programmes, e.g. news, documentaries, soap operas, comedy, chat shows, sport, children's programmes, films, plays, travel programmes
- programmes are educational
- helps you unwind
- prevents family arguments
- keeps the family together as a unit
- advertising informs
- censorship prevents unsuitability

3 🎤 Describing / spotting the differences / reaching a conclusion

Can competition (Groupwork for two or three students)

Part 3
In groups of two or three, look at the drawings at the top of the next page and decide:

- what kind of competition this might be.
- what you have to do to win it.
- who it might be aimed at.
- what message the pictures are trying to put across.
- whether you think they are successful in getting their message across.
- whether you can spot the differences!

Compare your decisions with those of another group.

Part 4
- What kind of prizes do you think might have been offered in the competition?
- What other things do we needlessly waste in our modern world?
- How can we educate people so that this type of wastage does not take place?
- How can supermarkets and shops help us with this problem of wastage?
- What will eventually happen if we take no notice at all of this problem?

4 Collaborating / selecting / reaching a conclusion

Save the stadium (Groupwork for two or three students)

You live near a stadium which was built for the last Olympic Games. Unfortunately it is losing money and in danger of being closed, unless it starts making a profit. Plan a series of events to bring in the crowds. Remember, you must raise as much money as possible!

Part 3
In groups of two or three decide:
- which three events suggested below would generate the biggest profits.
- which event you think would be the least popular.
- what you would charge for entry.
- what other entertainment or facilities you would provide, e.g. refreshments.
- what other activity you could suggest to raise money to save the stadium.

Part 4
- What attracts you personally to organized events?
- What problems have been caused by crowds at organized events? e.g football matches
- How can we control hundreds of people successfully?
- What's the difference between attending a 'live' event and watching it on TV?
- Name other reasons for trying to raise a lot of money.
- What other ways can you think of to raise money for a worthy cause?

Task bank 5C/D • Speaking

5 🎤 Collaborating / Matching / Expressing personal opinions

Installation art (Groupwork for two or three students)

Look at the pictures. Some people call them art, others a load of rubbish!

Part 3

In groups of two or three decide:
- which title would best fit each picture and why.
- where these art forms might be displayed.
- what ordinary people would think of them.
- how much you think it cost to produce them.
- which you like best and least.

Titles
- Lapwing, redwing, fieldfare
- This inability to escape
- Sight unseen
- Maid of the mist

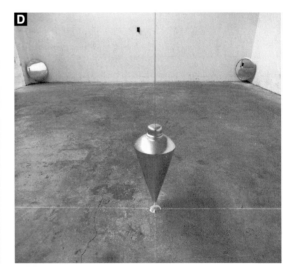

Part 4
- What kind of art do you like best?
- Have there been any famous artists in your own country? Who?
- If you were rich, would you sponsor a young but controversial artist?
- How do you think computers can change the face of art?
- Could you tell the difference between a reproduction and the 'real' thing?
- What kind of a person do you think you have to be to become an artist?

6 🎤 Collaborating / selecting / reaching a conclusion

Cheap city breaks (Groupwork for two or three students)

You work for a company organizing package weekend breaks to many major cities in the world. Recently, you have been losing business and you need to present your holidays in a new, more attractive way.

Part 3

In groups of two or three decide:

- which four cities below would be the most popular with people from the country you are living in at the moment.
- which four you could offer to your customers at a reasonable price.
- how you would transport customers to the cities you have chosen. Remember you have to keep the cost down, yet save time!
- what kind of accommodation you could offer customers in these cities.
- what optional excursions you could offer customers.
- how you would advertise or promote the holidays in order to generate more business.
- how you would beat your competitors.

Part 4

- What type of holidays are popular in your country?
- Why do we sometimes come back from a holiday thinking we need another one?
- What benefits do we get from visiting other countries for one or two weeks a year?
- What unexpected problems do we sometimes encounter while on holiday?
- Could you survive without an annual holiday? Why?

6 LISTENING

Paper 4 Task bank

Activities for Paper 4 Part 1

1 🎧 Sentence completion

Brooklyn Center schools' programs

You will hear part of a programme about America. As you listen, complete the sentences for questions 1–10 with an appropriate word or short phrase. (Notice the American spelling of *centre* and *programmes*.) You will hear the recording twice.

Schools' programs

Brooklyn Center for Urban Environment (BCUE) aims to help children find out about (1)_____ .

Designed for children of any (2)_____ .

Some children attending the BCUE have recently (3)_____ .

BCUE programs are quite (4)_____ .

Programs assist participants with many (5)_____ .

Teachers attend (6)_____ .

Adult and family audiences

(7)_____ tours popular with adult and family parties.

Events always have a different (8)_____ .

After-school programs

(9)_____ available for families with children age 4–14.

(10)_____ are part of the program.

Compare your answers with a partner before checking them.

Activities for Paper 4 Part 1 • **Task bank 6A**

2 🎧 Sentence completion
High-tech spy

You will hear part of a programme about a high-tech traffic spy. As you listen, complete the sentences for questions 1–9 with an appropriate word or short phrase. You will hear the recording twice.

The Automobile Club hopes the 'dirtiest' drivers will be exposed by the new (1)_____ .

Completion of the project has taken (2)_____ .

The new technology was developed in (3)_____ .

Identifying offending drivers now takes less than (4)_____ .

Speed cameras have resulted in a huge reduction in (5)_____ .

In some areas traffic violations have decreased by (6)_____ .

10% of motorists form a hardcore of (7)_____ .

Next month, tests will be carried out (8)_____ .

Highway patrols will be targeting (9)_____ .

Compare your answers with those of a partner before checking them.

3 🎧 Sentence completion
Artist's eye

You will hear part of a programme in which a doctor expresses a medical opinion about artists. As you listen, complete the sentences for questions 1–10 with an appropriate word or short phrase. You will hear the recording twice.

Artists who paint the world differently may have (1)_____ .

If you want to see blue clearly through brown sunglasses, you need to paint an extremely (2)_____ .

The fact that Claude Monet suffered from cataracts is apparent in (3)_____ .

In later life minor cataracts affect (4)_____ .

Monet suffered from a form of the disease which turned the eye lens (5)_____ .

In Monet's paintings of his garden, the whites are (6)_____ and the blues appear much (7)_____ .

In a fit of depression, Monet (8)_____ .

He never painted (9)_____ .

In 1922 he complained that everything he saw looked (10)_____ .

Three years after having cataract surgery, he (11)_____ .

In small groups compare your answers before checking them.

Task bank 6B • Listening

4 🎧 Sentence completion
Theme park

You will hear someone talking about theme parks and offering an 'unofficial' guide for first-time visitors. As you listen, complete the sentences for questions 1–11, with an appropriate word or short phrase. You will hear the recording twice.

Arrive before nine o'clock to avoid (1)_____ .

It's worth buying a ticket for (2)_____ .

Allow about an hour for (3)_____ and _____ .

The least awful gift shop is the one (4)_____ .

Younger children will enjoy the (5)_____ .

You needn't queue early to see the (6)_____ .

Small children will be terrified of (7)_____ .

The best time to buy souvenirs or gifts is (8)_____ .

Taking a (9)_____ saves you buying one there.

Rain does not affect (10)_____ .

Compared to Disney World it's (11)_____ .

Activities for Paper 4 Part 2

Material in this module focuses on extracting recycled information which is heard only once. However, an optional activity to give practice in note-taking could be carried out with a second listening.

1 🎧 Sentence completion
City robbery

You will hear a news report about some robbers whose pictures were captured on video. Complete the sentences for questions 1–9, using an appropriate word or short phrase. **Listen very carefully as you will hear the recording ONCE only.**

Robbers appear on video

The robbery occurred about a (1)_____ .

The distance between the camera and the jeweller's shop was (2)_____ .

The robbers made their getaway in (3)_____ .

Half an hour after the pictures were taken, the (4)_____ .

To avoid suspicion the men did not (5)_____ .

Commander Tucker thinks it will be possible to (6)_____ .

Compared to the first suspect, the passenger was both (7)_____.

The colour of the vehicle was (8)_____.

A warning about the robbery was received the (9)_____.

Compare your answers with those of a partner.

2 🎧 Sentence completion

Museum visit

You will hear a museum guide talking to a party of visitors to a museum. Complete the sentences for numbers 1–7, using an appropriate word or short phrase. **Listen very carefully as you will hear the recording ONCE only.**

New museum portrays both (1)_____.

Exhibits cover a historical period of (2)_____.

For centuries the area has enjoyed good (3)_____.

Local industries were helped by excellent means of (4)_____.

During your visit you meet some (5)_____.

All items in the display have been (6)_____.

Displays made more realistic by (7)_____.

In small groups, compare your answers before checking them in the key.

3 🎧 Note-taking

Baltic cruise

You will hear someone talking on a travel programme about a Baltic cruise. For questions 1–10, complete the sentences. **Listen very carefully as you will hear the recording ONCE only.**

Stockholm: 'The world's (1)_____'.

Cruises available from Stockholm to (2)_____.

Cruises organized by (3)_____.

Hotel in Stockholm situated (4)_____.

(5)_____ available on board the Northern Star for additional supplement.

Flights depart (6)_____ only.

Sunday spent in (7)_____.

Free time for (8)_____.

Monday night (9)_____ on board.

Phone quoting (10)_____.

Compare your answers with a partner before checking them in the key.

Task bank 6C • Listening

4 🎧 Sentence completion

National Asthma Campaign Open Day

You will hear the director of a charity, the National Asthma Campaign (NAC), welcoming participants and introducing speakers at an Open Day. For questions 1–9, complete the sentences. **Listen very carefully as you will hear the recording ONCE only.**

The Open Day is held every (1)_____ .

Those attending can find out more about current (2)_____ .

The NAC spent (3)_____ more on helping those with asthma than it did last year.

Only projects which have been vetted are considered for a (4)_____ .

People who have helped fight asthma ought to feel (5)_____ .

Lucy Wiggs is presenting the first paper instead of (6)_____ .

The first paper deals with children who suffer from (7)_____ .

The second paper focuses on sufferers of (8)_____ , particularly those living in (9)_____ .

With a partner, compare your answers before checking them in the key.

Activities for Paper 4 Part 3

1 🎧 Multiple choice questions

Hats

You will hear Paul Offord, the Managing Director, being interviewed about his family hat-making business. For questions 1–6, choose the correct option from **A**, **B**, **C** or **D**. You will hear the recording twice.

1. The company has been in existence
   A for more than 75 years.
   B since the late 1980s.
   C for the last five years.
   D since last year.

2. According to Paul, the company currently makes
   A 40,000 straw hats a year.
   B only panama hats.
   C hats for export only.
   D hundreds of different styles of hats.

3. He feels the future of the panama hat is
   A absolutely watertight.
   B somewhat uncertain.
   C rather gloomy.
   D reasonably secure.

4. The company felt it was necessary to
   A give big discounts to wholesalers.
   B sell directly to retailers.
   C open up branches in other countries.
   D close some of the branches in this country.

5. What does Paul regard as the company's main problem?
   A financing the manufacture of the hats
   B shipping hand-woven fibre from Ecuador
   C producing new styles for hats
   D storing hats before selling them

6. He thinks the main reason for the company's success is
   A being well-known in the high street.
   B manufacturing industrial headware.
   C the skill of its craftsmen.
   D recent cuts in staff numbers.

In small groups compare and justify your answers after listening once, then listen again and check to see if your first impressions were correct.

2 🎧 Multiple choice questions

Saving Australia

You will hear a travel writer talking to someone she is going to write an article about. For questions 1–9, choose the correct option from **A**, **B**, **C** or **D**. You will hear the recording twice.

1. How many of the state's forests have disappeared over the last century?
   A over a hundred
   B about three hundred
   C half the original number
   D probably millions

2. How much rain falls at this time of year in the region?
   A about three inches
   B a reasonable amount
   C half as much as England's annual rainfall
   D more than London's annual rainfall

3. What clothing does Cindy consider to be the most suitable for her work?
   A a T-shirt
   B waterproofs
   C wet clothes
   D no clothes

4. What was Cindy's dream?
   A to go to England
   B to be self-sufficient
   C to live on an island
   D to have children

5. Cindy originally travelled to Australia with
   A an English tourist.
   B a partner from America.
   C her two children.
   D some people in a commune.

6. How did the Australian owner feel about selling his property?
   A delighted
   B excited
   C unwilling
   D upset

7. Where did they sleep immediately after buying the property?
   A in an old farmhouse
   B out in the open
   C in a house she helped to build
   D under the shade of the trees

8. Cindy believes in living
   A somewhere isolated.
   B somewhere warm.
   C close to other human beings.
   D close to plants and animals.

9. What has become of the land?
   A It's covered in trees.
   B It's a holiday complex.
   C It houses several farms.
   D It's home to 20 people.

In pairs compare your answers after listening once, then listen again to see whether your first impressions were correct.

Task bank 6C • Listening

3 🎧 Two task types together

Two-star chef

For a really challenging task, try this activity with two different task types. If possible, listen once to answer each task type.
Alternately, one half of the class could try task one, the other half task two, then you can see who does best!
You will hear a food critic, Andrea, talking to a famous chef.

A Multiple choice questions

For questions 1–9 choose the correct option from **A**, **B**, **C** or **D**.

1 What is Marco Pierre well-known for?
  A sacking staff
  B making staff feel small
  C being enthusiastic
  D being the best chef in the country

2 How does he think his appearance has changed over the last eight years?
  A His hair is longer.
  B His complexion is less clear.
  C He weighs a lot more.
  D He wears different clothes.

3 How does he usually treat his customers nowadays?
  A He throws many out of his restaurant.
  B He fights with many of them.
  C He makes jokes at their expense.
  D He makes them laugh.

4 He asked one food critic to leave
  A in front of the man's guest.
  B when he met the man in the bathroom.
  C without paying his bill.
  D in the middle of lunch.

5 How does he treat his kitchen staff nowadays?
  A He bullies them mercilessly.
  B He keeps them under control.
  C He takes advantage of them.
  D He shouts at them unnecessarily.

6 The 'two-star' chef spent his childhood in
  A Leeds.
  B Chelsea.
  C Knightsbridge.
  D Italy.

7 What is the code he lives by?
  A He forgives people who apologize.
  B He criticizes people face to face.
  C He forgives and forgets everything.
  D He never speaks ill of anybody.

8 What does he believe?
  A arrogance is a negative quality
  B arrogance creates success
  C greatness does not follow success
  D arrogance is created by greatness

9 What did Andrea think of the meal she had?
  A There was too much to eat.
  B It wasn't simple enough.
  C The chef's ability had been exaggerated.
  D She had never tasted a meal like it.

In pairs, try to justify your answers before making your final decision.

B Identify the comments the speakers make

During the interview Andrea and Marco make various comments. For questions 1–13 indicate which comments are made by Andrea and which by Marco by writing

　A (for Andrea)
　M (for Marco)
or N (for neither).

  1 Marco was originally an accountant.
  2 The Michelin Guide awarded Marco stars when he was in his 20s.
  3 Marco has 'expanded' in more ways than one!
  4 Marco appears in the restaurant itself a few times a week.

5 Marco frightens some of the customers.
6 Customers no longer come looking for a fight.
7 Food critics often make personal attacks on chefs.
8 Rival chefs are considered enemies.
9 Marco has a slight regional accent.
10 Marco only employs strong people.
11 Marco doesn't let people forget what they've done to him.
12 Marco is pleased with his success.
13 The next step for Marco is retirement.

In small groups, compare your answers before checking them in the key.

4 Two task types together

Touring holiday

Here is another task with two different task types. If possible, listen once to answer each task type.
Alternatively, one half of the class could try task one, the other half task two, then you can see who does better!
You will hear someone talking to tourists travelling around Europe.

A Multiple choice questions

For questions 1–8 choose the correct option from **A**, **B**, **C** or **D**.

1 Who would have preferred to stay in places longer?
 A Janey
 B Gary
 C Oliver
 D all three

2 Who wanted to see Michelangelo's *David* again?
 A Janey
 B Gary
 C Oliver
 D all three

3 What had Gary never been able to eat before coming to Europe?
 A cheese
 B apples
 C herbs
 D white chocolate

4 What did Janey miss most about home?
 A cola
 B wine
 C ice
 D McDonald's

5 Now Janey thinks most Europeans are
 A an unfriendly lot of people.
 B not interested in Americans.
 C only interested in money.
 D pleasant, helpful people.

6 What reason is given for Americans spending only short holidays in Europe?
 A lack of money
 B a desire to see other continents
 C short vacations
 D family commitments at home

7 How did Gary and Janey prepare for their trip?
 A They bought guide books before they left.
 B They read guide books on the plane.
 C They read as much as possible about Europe.
 D They did not have time to do anything.

8 What did Janey find in Munich that she couldn't find at home?
 A souvenir coffee spoons
 B clothes for older women
 C leather bags
 D crystal

In pairs, try to justify your choice before making your final decision.

Task bank 6D • Listening

B Identify the comments the speakers make

For questions 1–15 indicate which comments are made by Janey, which by Gary and which by Oliver by writing
   J (for Janey)
   G (for Gary)
or O (for Oliver).

Do not refer to your answers for Task A above!

1. I got to know the real Europe.
2. I would like to have spent longer in one or two places.
3. I'd like to see France again.
4. I was able to eat chocolate in Switzerland.
5. It was disappointing to find food with chemical additives.
6. There's a world of difference between fresh herbs and dried herbs.
7. The thing I liked most was the ice cream.
8. We paid only one visit to McDonald's.
9. The hotel staff weren't very friendly.
10. Most Americans lead a busy life.
11. Time is more important than money to Europeans.
12. We just ate and drank on the plane.
13. It's difficult to find nice souvenir coffee spoons at home.
14. I couldn't buy anything because the shops were closed.
15. Europeans don't have big cars because the streets aren't wide enough.

In small groups check to see whether you have put the appropriate letter in the correct place. It's sometimes easy to know the answer but make a mistake with the task type.

Which task did you find more challenging? Why?

Activities for Paper 4 Part 4

For this part of the exam you will hear the recording only once for each task.

1 Multiple matching

Relationships

You will hear various people talking about relationships.

Task one

For questions 1–5, match the extracts as you hear them with the people the speakers are referring to, listed A–H.

A a colleague
B an acquaintance
C a fiancé(e)
D a grandparent
E a boss
F a best friend
G a son / daughter
H a husband / wife

	1
	2
	3
	4
	5

In small groups, compare your answers before going on to the next task.

Activities for Paper 4 Part 4 • **Task bank 6C**

Task two

For questions 6–10, match the extracts as you hear them with the attitudes of the speakers listed A–H.

A resentful
B furious
C frustrated
D pessimistic
E nostalgic
F affectionate
G cheerful
H resigned

6
7
8
9
10

In the same small groups, compare your answers before checking them.

2 🎧 Two task types at the same time
Class distinction

Divide the class into two groups. The first group can try task A and the second task B. See which group does better!

A Multiple matching

You will hear various people talking about class distinction.

Task one

For questions 1–5, match the extracts as you hear them with the people listed A–J. (There are more options than in the exam!)

A a financier
B a head of state
C a factory worker
D an artist
E a single parent
F an industrialist
G an aristocrat
H an unmarried mother
I a landscape gardener
J a computer consultant

1
2
3
4
5

This time, go straight into the next task without comparing your answers – as you would have to in the exam!

Task two

For questions 6–10, match the extracts as you hear them with the comments listed A–I. (There are more options than in the exam!)

A The family unit is under threat.
B There is no snobbery in this country.
C Mum and dad interfere.
D I'm afraid to meet people.
E I have no social life.
F I regret not studying more.
G My children go to a private school.
H A sophisticated accent is a drawback.
I You decide your own future.

6
7
8
9
10

Now compare your answers for both tasks with those of a partner before checking them.

Task bank 6D • Listening

B Multiple choice

You will hear five different speakers. As you listen, choose the correct option **A**, **B** or **C**.

Speaker 1
1 The first speaker attributes her own success to
 A her education.
 B her determination.
 C her upbringing.

2 She considers the most important thing in life to be
 A a stable family life.
 B a satisfying job.
 C a comfortable existence.

Speaker 2
3 The second speaker wishes
 A he hadn't studied art.
 B he had been more talented.
 C he hadn't left school so soon.

4 He now works
 A as an artist.
 B in a factory.
 C for a film producer.

Speaker 3
5 The third speaker spent her childhood
 A in Liverpool.
 B in the south west.
 C away from her parents.

6 She would really like to
 A help her mum and dad.
 B own a TV.
 C go out more.

Speaker 4
7 The fourth speaker says that the most important thing about people is
 A what they do for a living.
 B their family background.
 C what they are like.

8 He is sometimes self-conscious about
 A the kind of job he does.
 B the way he speaks.
 C entering a crowded room.

Speaker 5
9 The fifth speaker thinks problems in his country are caused by
 A the weakening of the family unit.
 B class distinction.
 C people's feelings of superiority.

10 He says that having a title nowadays
 A gives one status.
 B is problematic.
 C brings money and privilege.

3 Multiple matching

Food

You will hear various people talking about food.

Task one

For questions 1–5, match the extracts as you hear them with the people A–H.

A a food critic
B a zoo-keeper
C a fitness instructor
D a marine biologist
E a psychiatrist
F a book reviewer
G an anthropologist
H a reporter

1
2
3
4
5

This time, go straight into the next task without a longer pause – as you would have to in the exam.

Task two

For questions 6–10, match the extracts as you hear them with the aspects of food the people are talking about, listed A–H.

A a different type of diet
B evolutionary changes in eating habits
C eating disorders
D the problems of over-indulgence
E observing eating behaviour
F the over-production of food
G supply and demand
H contaminated food supplies

	6
	7
	8
	9
	10

Now compare your answers for both tasks with those of a partner before checking them.

4 🎧 Multiple matching

Coping with the unexpected

You will hear various people talking about unexpected things which happened to them.

Task one

For questions 1–5, match the extracts as you hear them with the places where these things happened, listed A–H.

A a cinema
B an aeroplane
C a restaurant
D a lift
E a riverbank
F a take-away cafe
G an underground train
H a stadium

	1
	2
	3
	4
	5

After listening once, compare your answers with those of a partner.

Task two

For questions 6–10, match the extracts as you hear them with the unexpected happenings listed A–H.

A a clumsy accident
B simulated reality
C a physical injury
D a misunderstanding
E a disagreement
F a strange coincidence
G an electrical fault
H inclement weather

	6
	7
	8
	9
	10

Compare your answers with those of the same partner before checking them.

Pairwork

Page 48 **Exam Practice**

Student A – INFORMATION CARD

- height
- colour of eyes
- any brothers / sisters
- job experience
- favourite food
- favourite entertainment
- greatest ambition

Page 86 **Job application**

Student B

You are the personnel officer at the University of Glamorgan in Wales. Someone wants to speak to you about a job abroad. You have the advertisement for the job in front of you. Answer the person's questions as politely and patiently as possible and give any other information which you feel will be useful.

English Language Adviser

BEIJING, CHINA

Salary: £20,000 p.a inc. + benefits package

We wish to appoint an experienced English Language Adviser to be seconded to an overseas study centre in Beijing, China.

The overseas study centre is to establish a foundation year designed to raise the English Language study skills of students to enable them to study in an English-medium University. The postholder will be responsible for establishing the project. This will involve course design, planning and assisting teacher-training / development programmes.

Candidates should hold an M.A. in Applied English Linguistics, or equivalent, and should possess a minimum of 6 years' relevant EFL experience. A knowledge of Mandarin would be a strong advantage.

This appointment is initially for one year.

University of Glamorgan

Appointments
We operate a no smoking policy
Application forms and further particulars may be obtained from:

The Personnel Services Division
University of Glamorgan
Pontypridd, Mid Glamorgan CF37 1DL

Telephone: 0443 482021 (Direct Line – 24 hour service)

Working towards equality of opportunity

Pairwork

Pages 86–87 **Insurance policy**

Student B

You are working on a commission basis for an insurance company and you have to do business to make money. Answer your client's questions as politely and patiently as possible and try to persuade your client that the policy is a good one.

TRAVEL INSURANCE

We consider Holiday Insurance to be essential if you are travelling abroad and believe that everyone should have at least Personal Insurance Cover.

The Holiday Insurance schemes we offer have been arranged by Hamilton Barr Insurance Brokers Ltd., and are underwritten at Lloyds. A brief summary of the cover provided is outlined below, but, should you wish to see full details of cover, we will be pleased to send you a copy of the wording, on application. Otherwise, full details of cover will be sent to you with your confirmation invoice.

Personal Insurance – summary of cover

- Personal accident – £5,000
- Medical and other expenses – £250,000
- Hospitalisation benefit – £10 per day (£300 in total)
- Cancellation and curtailment – £1,000
- Travel delay – £100
- Disruption of public transport – £200
- Baggage – £750
- Cash – £200
- Public liability – £1,000,000
- Legal expenses – £10,000

Vehicle breakdown and recovery insurance

This insurance will enable you to continue your holiday if your car breaks down or is involved in an accident. Therefore, you may also like to consider this type of cover in order to minimise the extent to which your holiday could be disrupted.

Please note that, in common with all other insurances of this type, this insurance does not cover the cost of repairs (other than emergency repairs, as mentioned above) and replacement parts.

Premiums

PERIOD	ADULTS	CHILDREN	VEHICLE
Up to 5 days	£8.00	£4.00	£18.00
Up to 10 days	£10.00	£5.00	£23.00
Up to 18 days	£13.00	£6.50	£28.00
Additional weeks	£3.00	£1.50	£5.00

- Infants under 2 years of age are insured free
- • Vehicles must not be over 10 years of age

Pairwork

Page 87 Mail order query

Student B

You ordered some free CDs from a mail order company a few weeks ago and they have still not arrived. Fortunately you have kept a photocopy of the order form stating which CDs you ordered. Talk to an employee of the firm and tell them what they need to know.

SEND NO MONEY NOW!

0196 To: Anglia Music Club, Freepost, Camberwell, London.
Yes! Please accept me as a member and send me the following 3 recordings on 10 day home trial.

5159   5899   3254   (enter selection numbers here)

COMPACT DISCS ✓   CASSETTES ☐   (please tick one box only, we cannot supply a mixed despatch)

I can audition the 3 recordings on approval. You will only invoice me for the price of one at £12.99 for compact discs or £8.49 for cassettes (plus £1.96 towards postage, packing and insurance for all 3). If not completely satisfied, I will return all 3 recordings undamaged within 10 days of receipt, my membership will be cancelled, and I will owe nothing.

Please also send my Welcome Magazine and Member's Handbook. As a member, I agree to buy at least 3 Regular Price recordings per year, for the first two years only. This is my only commitment. I am not obliged to order every month.

If I do not wish to receive the Editor's top recommendation I may say so on the order form provided.

My favourite kind of music is:
Pop 3 ☐   Rock 4 ☐   Easy Listening 2 ☐   Classical 1 ☐   (Please tick one box only)

Mr / Mrs / Miss / Ms
Address
Postcode
(I am over 18)
Signature

We regret this coupon cannot be accepted without signature. Important: Have you ticked the Compact Disc/Cassette box?
FREEPOST ★ NO STAMP NEEDED ★ 10 DAY HOME TRIAL
Offer closes 30.9.92. All orders subject to acceptance. One membership per household only. Please allow up to 28 days for delivery. Offer applies in UK, Channel Isles and BFPO only. Postage, packing and insurance charges quoted are based on rates at time of going to press and may vary.

A Anglia   BRITAIN'S MUSIC CLUB

5159

5899

3254

Pairwork

Page 87 **Holiday villa**

Student B

You own a villa which you rent out to holidaymakers in the Mediterranean area. You are talking to a potential client who has not seen your advertisement for the villa. Answer the queries as patiently and politely as possible.

Costa Blanca
VILLA ROSA

Accommodates 8 comfortably (4–6 in low season)

Villa Rosa is a spacious old farmhouse which has been beautifully restored. Set in its own fenced garden of 2000 sq.m. surrounded by orange and lemon groves. Private pool. 1km from Pedreguer for supermarkets, services and medical centre, and 15 minutes to Javea and Denia for beaches etc.

Accommodation: one double, three twin bedded bedrooms (one en-suite with own terrace), two other bathrooms and terraces. Large well furnished lounge, dining room, well fitted kitchen with microwave, magi-mix, fridge, freezer, etc. Utility room with washing machine. Barbecue and lots of garden furniture.

Low season – the owners live in the villa during low season and make available a completely self-contained upper apartment (sleeping 4 – 6) at specially reduced rates.

Tel: 0181 928 4820

Property rental prices per week

LOW SEASON * Oct – May	MID SEASON June – Sept	HIGH SEASON July – Aug
Special reduced terms	£500	£650

Apartment only available during low season

Pairwork

Page 88 Leisure complex enquiry
Student B

You work at the information desk at a leisure complex. Talk to a potential customer and answer their queries as patiently and politely as possible using the information in this leaflet.

BARNET QUASAR
SERIOUS FUN WITH A LASER GUN

- A tremendous, safe, non-contact game bringing sophisticated laser technology to the masses, and played in a futuristic high-tech arena

- Open until late, every night

- Advance bookings taken or just turn up and join the next available game

- General prices from £8 – £9 per person per half hour session. No extras!

- League action; weekly Top Gun prizes; individual and family membership schemes

- 7 game formats to choose from. A 30 laser system featuring red and green beams

CHILDREN'S EVENTS
Special events laid on for children's birthdays etc. Suitable for age 7 and over. Quasar really does make a birthday extra special!

CORPORATE EVENTS
Improve your team's performance. For a corporate event that will definitely be memorable, we can arrange total exclusivity with refreshments and light snacks, if required.

CHARITY EVENTS
As a fundraiser, Quasar has few equals. We can sit down and work out a mutually acceptable formula.

We can accommodate exclusive bookings from 10 people to 150 or more. For any kind of party Quasar at Barnet provides stunning excitement.

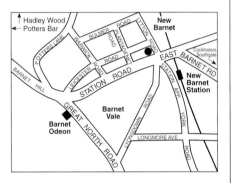

**THE BARNET QUASAR CENTRE
LYTTON ROAD, BARNET
'SERIOUS FUN' INFORMATION LINE 081 440 0540.**

Page 48 Exam Practice
Student B – INFORMATION CARD

- place of birth
- weight
- present occupation
- favourite actor / actress
- secret wish
- favourite drink
- reason for studying English

Identity parade page 15

Describing a re-enactment page 74

Pairwork

Possible suspects page 88

Colourful events page 89

Pairwork

Ball control
page 89

Modern sculpture
page 89

Outdoor entertainment page 89

Pairwork

Building development pages 89–90

February 1989

Street market page 90

Pairwork

Kitchens page 90

Art forms page 90

Pairwork

People on the telephone page 90

China figures page 91

Pairwork

Identity parade page 15

Describing a re-enactment page 74

Ball control
page 89

Modern sculpture
page 89

Pairwork

Outdoor entertainment page 89

Climbing page 88

People on the telephone page 90

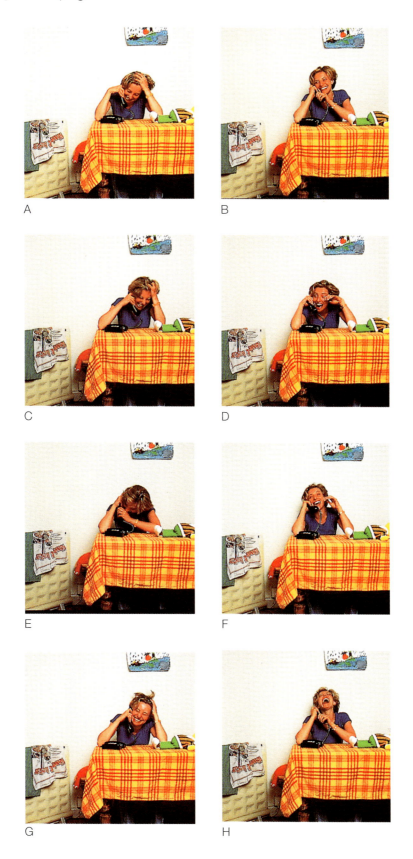

Pairwork

China figures page 91

TAPESCRIPTS

1 SPEAKING

1A Getting to know you

2.0 page 7

A **B**=Mr Black, **W**=Miss Williams, **S**=Students
B I'm Mr Black and I would like to introduce you both to my colleague Miss Williams.
S How do you do?
W How do you do?

B **J**=Jane, **B**=Barry, **S**=Students
J Hello. I'm Jane Watson and this is my colleague Barry Jones.
S Good morning.
   Hello.
B Hello.

C **M**=Mary, **J**=John, **S**=Students
M I'm Mary and this is John.
S Hi!
   Hi there!
J Hello.

3.0 page 8

Good morning. I'm Charles Young and I'm going to be teaching you Information Technology for this term. Some of you may know me already – in fact I recognize one or two faces from the Computer Systems course I ran last year. I've been teaching in the college for the last four years – and, by the way, I also run the college drama group! So if there are any budding actors or actresses out there please see me in the break! Now, if there are any questions . . .

4.1 page 9

1 A And your surname?
   B The name is Hart.
2 A What was the name again, please?
   B Welt, Frank Welt.
3 A And you're Mary . . .
   B Manton.
   A Oh, yes. Manton.
4 A And the address?
   B 14, Gracelands Road.
   A 14, Gracelands Road.
5 A What was the name of that company again.
   B Roland Motors.
   A Roland Motors?
   B That's right.
6 A You did say Pond Street, didn't you?
   B I certainly did. Pond as in duck!
   A Yes . . .

1B People and places

2.0 page 12

Last night police issued this description of a woman believed to have been involved in an armed robbery in a high street bank in the city yesterday afternoon. She was slim, in her twenties, of medium height, with long, dark hair. She had big blue eyes and was wearing a long trench coat type mackintosh, and carrying a large, black shoulder bag. She had flat shoes on and was wearing long dangling earrings and had a small diamond ring on the little finger of her left hand.

2.2 page 14

The National Savings Bank in Kingston High Street was the target of an armed robbery at around 2.30 this afternoon. A woman had entered the National Savings Bank in Kingston at 2.27, three minutes before the robbery took place. She is believed to have been an accomplice of the gang who attacked and robbed a security firm delivering £15,000 in cash to the premises. She was noticed by several customers who were in the bank at the time because she went straight to the front of the queue, gave something to two men waiting there, then left immediately. About three minutes later, just as the security firm were making their afternoon delivery at 2.30, the two men who had been waiting in the queue produced machine guns and forced the security guards and the customers to lie face-down on the floor while they made their escape with the £15,000 cash. Bank staff eventually raised the alarm but it was too late. The gang of three had already made off in a car parked illegally outside the bank, and driven by the woman who had previously entered the bank at 2.27.
A traffic warden, who was writing out a parking ticket when the robbers came running out of the bank and drove off in the car at high speed, was able to give police a detailed description of all three robbers.

1C/D Jobs and training

2.1 page 18

R=Reporter, **M**=Dr Marlow
R Academic excellence has brought its own rewards for Dr Simon Marlow, who in 1986 joined the transatlantic 'brain drain'.
   Now, at 32, and still single, he is Assistant Professor of Mathematics at the University of Chicago. He rents a flat on the edge of the city, enjoys the climate and uses his jeep to explore.
   However, sailing through his advanced level exams proved easier than recalling the subjects involved when I talked to him recently.
M I can remember . . . er . . . six, I think, er, six advanced level passes with grade A. I know pure maths was one of them . . . hum . . . I'm not doing very well, am I?
R Well, since you entered the record books with *seven* grade A passes in 1978, well, no, you're not! Would you say that you were a child prodigy – a genius when you were at school?
M They never thought I was going to do anything worthwhile at primary school. They thought I was a bit vague. But I proved them wrong!
R I have it on record that when you got your A level results the computer rejected them.
M That's right! They had to be done again by hand! My mother was the one who was most impressed. She said it was lovely having a son who was such a prodigy and she couldn't wait to tell everybody!
R So, armed with your astonishing results you chose Essex university . . .
M Yes, er, it had an excellent reputation for maths and computing, both of which I wanted to study for my degree . . .
R . . . but after that you went to . . .
M . . . to Oxford
R . . . where you did a doctorate in maths, in . . . 1981?
M Yes, but when I finished in 1986 the money offered to me in America proved impossible to resist. Still, I watch the debate on education with great interest. I'm against studying a wider range of subjects, myself. If I'd been forced to study arts I'd never have got anywhere. We should let people specialize in what they're good at.
R And do you still keep in touch with your friends back home?
M Certainly. I use my computerised electronic mail system, and I listen to the BBC!
R And do you think you'll ever come back to England?
M After you've been somewhere for a while it becomes almost as hard to come back. I'm not really very good at making big decisions. I let things happen to me!

129

Tapescripts • Module 2A

2.3 page 19

F=father, **S**=son

F Well, you know what they say: hard work brings its own *rewards*!
S Hmn . . . I suppose there might be *a grain* of truth in what you say.
F Don't *hedge* . . . you know I'm right really!
S Yes! . . . I'm just *recoiling* in horror at the thought of all this hard work!
F Oh, you *poor* thing!
S Do I get the *vague* idea that you're being sarcastic? Anyway, it's not that . . . It's just that I'm not sure I *believe* in work for its own sake.
F Don't look so *dejected*. You know I can't *resist* teasing you!
S Well, you've certainly hit the *nail* on the head there!

2 LISTENING

2A Sorry, I didn't quite catch that!

1.0 page 23

Various background sounds: see key on page 146.

1.1 page 24

1 I'm speaking to you from the main runway where a few flights are still operating.
2 Actually we're in an emergency phone box on the motorway.
3 Hey! What do you think you're doing to my car?
4 This is a staff announcement. Could Andrew Sinclair please come to the customer service desk at the front of the store?
5 And the crowd are going wild here – with only two minutes left to go.
6 Go on, go on! Go and fetch it Rover!

2.0 page 24

1 Prices these days, I ask you. Shocking. Even going down to the shops for half a pound of butter nearly breaks the old piggy bank – know what I mean? We should never've gone decimal. We should've kept the old pounds, shillings and pence!
2 People ask what it's like to live down under and I always say the same thing. It's probably like living anywhere else but the climate's better – sun 'n' surf! Just a pity it's such a long way for you Europeans!
3 But it's a beautiful country – you've got to come over and see it for yourself! Sure, it rains but that's why it so green! And the scenery – to tell the truth, we're better off without too many tourists. It would only spoil what mother nature's given us!
4 I guess people have this strange idea that we're convinced we're bigger and better than anyone else. I can't say for sure about better, but bigger? It sure is a big country you're talking about here. You only realise *how* big when you're driving from east to west!
5 People don't always realise we've got the oldest language in Europe. Oh, they come looking for mountains and scenery. We've got plenty of that, mind you! But we've got a very old and ancient culture, and some of the best singers in the world!

2.1 page 24

Possible key words are in **bold**.

1 I mean to say, people are being **turfed out** of their **homes** – and all because the government have decided to **build** this new **link road**.
2 Imagine taking to the **skies** and **floating** gently across the open **countryside** in a **wicker basket** – you can see for **miles** and miles.
3 The Bisell Magic **broom** must be one of the most **versatile upright vacuum cleaners** on the **market** today. It can do in **seconds** what it might take you **hours** to do **by hand**.
4 The **society** has been **in the red** for six months now, and **auditors** say that its **financial future** looks **insecure**.
5 During our three-day **trip** to **Holland**, you will be taken on a **full-day excursion** to the **Dutch bulb fields** to visit the world-**famous nurseries**.

3.0 page 25

See key on page 147.

4.0 page 26

First reading

A retired grocer, Roland Bloom, was ordered by a court yesterday to pay local council taxes on his village shop. Mr Bloom, aged 96, was said yesterday evening to be devastated as his shop has been closed since 1980. However, it has been lovingly preserved as a time capsule of the fifties. Magistrates in Liskeard, Cornwall, heard that Mr Bloom owed back-taxes on his shop. The premises had been assessed as a non-domestic property, and the shop, established by his father in 1902, has remained virtually untouched since its closure, and is still lit by gas light. Although closed to the public, it occupies the ground floor of Mr Bloom's three-storey town house. Mr Bloom has refused to dismantle it because he's considering bequeathing it intact to the village as a museum. Yesterday Mr Bloom said, 'I'm very cross. It hasn't been used as a shop for years and it's unfair.'

Second reading

1 A retired grocer, Roland Bloom, was ordered by a court yesterday to pay local council taxes on his village shop.
2 Mr Bloom, aged 96, was said yesterday evening to be devastated as his shop has been closed since 1980.
3 However, it has been lovingly preserved as a time capsule of the fifties.
4 Magistrates in Liskeard, Cornwall, heard that Mr Bloom owed back-taxes on his shop.
5 The premises had been assessed as a non-domestic property.
6 The shop, established by his father in 1902, has remained virtually untouched since its closure.
7 It is still lit by gas light.
8 Although closed to the public, it occupies the ground floor of Mr Bloom's three-storey town house.
9 Mr Bloom has refused to dismantle it because he's considering bequeathing it intact to the village as a museum.
10 Yesterday Mr Bloom said, 'I'm very cross. It hasn't been used as a shop for years and it's unfair.'

Exam practice page 28

R=Reporter, **L**=Ernie Lawson, **G**=David Gurney

R A 69-year-old farmer, Ernie Lawson, has found himself caught in a dilemma. Yesterday, he was ordered by a court to hand over his stunning find last month of thousands of gold and silver coins, brooches, spoons and statues dating from AD 383. Mr Lawson, who discovered the hoard with his metal detector and had to scoop up his treasure into supermarket plastic bags, was devastated when we talked to him yesterday evening. Despite his plea that his discovery is of great historical importance, and was made on his land – and his insistence that he informed the authorities of his find as soon as he discovered it – magistrates have ordered Mr Lawson to hand every single object over to the authorities or face the possibility of prosecution.
Lawson found his treasure, which has remained more or less intact since it was placed there all those years ago, while he was looking for some farm tools. The find, none of which Mr Lawson will be allowed to keep, is said to be worth about £10 million pounds but Mr Lawson may only receive compensation for those objects he dug up himself. Most of the objects were actually uncovered by a team of archaeologists, who later came to excavate the site.
Yesterday evening Mr Lawson was in a belligerent mood:
L To be honest, I'm very cross and, naturally, disappointed. It certainly won't encourage me, or anybody else with a metal detector, to come forward and declare our discoveries in future, I can tell you!
R We also talked to David Gurney, principal archaeologist for the Museum in the area.
G Yes, certainly, we do sympathize with Mr Lawson. We know about 200 people who are only too delighted to go over a field with their metal detectors for us. The finds can be well, just absolutely staggering. We estimate that over the last decade more than 300,000 objects've been brought to museums by metal-detecting enthusiasts. But this find's of particular importance because it lay buried in a field which wasn't even considered a likely archaeological site.
It's time we acknowledged the value of the hobby of metal detecting and said a proper 'thank you' to all those who help to enrich our museums. Of course, they ought to be entitled to proper compensation, too. But the law's the law and, well, maybe that's what we've really got to change!
R An official decision on the treasure trove is expected some time in the next few days.

2B Leisure activities and holidays

1.1 page 29

B=Boy, **G**=Girl

B You certainly wouldn't catch me pot-holing – I can't think of anything more terrifying than being stuck underground, wondering whether the whole lot's going to come tumbling down on top of my head!

G Oh, come on! It's not that bad! Actually, it's not really that dangerous if you know what you're doing. Certainly no worse than, say . . . er . . . bungee jumping!

B Cor, only a lunatic would try that. Did you hear about that couple who jumped off a bridge, in Australia, I think, to celebrate their wedding. They actually jumped together! I ask you! . . . I'm not one for these mad escapades. My idea of exercise is a nice quiet stroll along the seashore on a spring afternoon with my dog . . .

G Not very adventurous, are you?

B Look who's talking! The most exciting thing that you've ever done is aerobics!

G What?

1.3 page 30

M=Man, **W**=Woman

M Well, today's programme is entitled Boredom Busters! If it's boring in Goring, or you're cheesed off in Cheshire, don't despair. We're here to rescue you with loads of holiday activities all over the country!
When it comes to hobbies, you could always add another string to your bow and take up archery. It's bang on target for summer fun! If you live in Birmingham you can join the Bowman archery club. Other members include the country's junior champions. There are at least two sessions each week and it's only £1 a time to chance your arm! Phone after 4 pm.
If that doesn't turn you on, then there are more than 100 bird sanctuaries organised by the Society for the Protection of Birds. Grab your binoculars and head for Swindon, where you can see a huge variety of birds, as well as red deer, water voles and even otters. That's a great day out at Swindon for only £3. The number's in the phone book and you can phone during office hours! Don't try phoning outside office hours as they don't have an answering machine and you might disturb the wild-life!
If you've ever had a yearning to be a member of a synchronized swimming team, Bristol has a synchronized swimming club. Three of its members have competed in the Olympics. For a modest fee and a £17 annual subscription you can join them! You can try it out without the annual subscription but once you've got the bug, £17 will seem like good value for money! For more information send a stamped addressed envelope to the programme. We'll give you our address to put on your envelope later. Please don't forget to include your address and a stamp – without it we'll be unable to send you the information. Judy, over to you.

W Well, some sports centres now have their own climbing wall – which means you've got a mountain on your doorstep just waiting to be scaled! You can try climbing on one of the activity days at Southport Centre. They cost only £16 a day and, although £16 may seem a lot at the time, there's a chance to have a go at loads of other ace sports throughout the day including sailing, shooting and ski-ing. Write in for details.
And finally, why not join a ballroom dancing team? Get into step and you'll have a ball doing the cha-cha-cha and you may even become a champion! Middlesex sports complex offers ballroom dancing lessons for only £2.50 a session, so if you live in the Middlesex area write in for details. No previous experience is necessary.
So that's it for today. For loads more activity ideas tune into Boredom Busters tomorrow at 5.30. Now for those addresses we promised you.

2.0 page 30

See key on page 147.

2.1 page 31

M=Man, **W**=Woman

M How do you fancy getting away from it all for half the price you would normally pay? The *Daily Telegraph* can help you! To take up this exclusive offer of two nights' hotel accommodation for the price of one at more than 450 superb hotels, all you need to do is collect the tokens published in the *Daily Telegraph* between August 14th and September 6th and attach them to special collector cards.

W When you have collected sufficient tokens, you can claim two consecutive nights' bed and breakfast for two people for the price of one at any of the participating hotels. If you complete both the collector cards, you can take advantage of this offer a second time.

M Every day from August 14th until Monday September 6th the *Daily Telegraph* will publish one token in each copy of the newspaper. All you need to do is collect ten differently numbered tokens and stick them in spaces provided on your collector card. The first collector card was published last Saturday, the second is published in today's issue of the *Daily Telegraph*.

W You may use your collector card any time between September the 1st and May the 31st (subject to individual hotels) and remember, if you collect 20 tokens you can fill both collector cards and enjoy two short breaks. Wherever you decide to go, you'll be sure of a glorious time!

3.0 page 31

Is your idea of having a ball leaving all your troubles behind you and travelling around under your own steam? If so, the Kon-Tiki 640 motorcaravan might suit you very well!

3.1 page 31

R=Reporter, **J**=Rick Jenkins

R Motorcaravanners are known as 'luggers' in the caravan world – people who lug their living quarters around with them. They don't mind that. In fact, they're happy to be recognised as a different breed! They have a word for the caravan lot as well: 'tuggers'. The luggers are well in the minority, with about 100,000 registered vehicles in the UK compared with well over half a million caravans.
Both camps are officially on good terms, but there is a trace of unease in the alliance. In the early days of motorcaravanning, back in the 60s, the Caravan Club wouldn't allow luggers to join, and banned them from their sites.
Hostilities have officially ceased now. Motorcaravans are welcome, provided, in the words of the Caravan Club code, their 'appearance is appropriate and does not offend public opinion'.
However, before getting carried away, buyers are advised to ask themselves some questions about how they are going to use their motorcaravan before making their choice. Then they should hire one for an experimental weekend.
The first question is, will it be the only family car, used for school trips and shopping as well as camping trips? If so, it will need to be small, not too thirsty on fuel and low enough to get into supermarket and municipal car parks!
But for Rick Jenkins, who retired at 43 by building up a steel construction business and selling it, only a full-blown model will do! He and his wife Linda enjoy a separate bedroom area, sitting room, TV, video, air conditioning, bathroom, bar, microwave and central heating!

J We want to see the world while living in the style we've become accustomed to at home.

R As the luggers' motto, that might do!

Exam practice page 33

Is tourism forging an even closer union of peoples, or is it, perhaps, achieving the reverse? It's well-known, for instance, what people think about some of the German tourists they've met on holiday: some've been known to take possession of the grounds of their hotel by throwing their towels over deck chairs and poolsides from as early as 7 o'clock in the morning to stake their claim!
What do the Germans think of other nationalities, though? And each of everyone else? Each nation has its own perception of the other, and, at the risk of generalization, some observations can be made about what we think of foreigners!
People tend to think of the Dutch as good solid fellows: decent and unassuming. But when they descend upon the German autobahns, at the start of their long journey south, the Germans can't believe how slowly many Dutch cars travel: the 'Dutch snail's pace', as it's called, so slow is their progress sometimes! And by the time they, and the Belgians, get to Spain, it's a standing Spanish joke that both nationalities are often incapable of negotiating the mountain roads or handling their cars on the steep slopes so unfamiliar in their own countries!
The French are sometimes thought to be rather proud, as they're known to be a little critical

about the food in the countries they visit. After all, nobody cooks better than the French!

The British have a dual reputation. There are the nasty characters in shorts with red, peeling, sunburnt skin all over their bodies, then there's the great mass of British travellers who are very long-suffering and never very demonstrative, and who sit there chewing sadly over their food without complaining or grumbling about anything.

When the Italians venture from Italy, they can be seen driving in search of far-distant green places on the edge of the British Isles. It's very fashionable in Italy to say that you've been to Scotland! Scotland's almost become a status symbol!

And the Americans, well . . . ! Although they do seem to be in a hurry, they always seem to find time for an amicable chat. They're generally regarded as being open and friendly, despite the fact that, according to them, everything is always bigger and better at home!

As for the Japanese, no tour would be complete unless each member of the group had a camera. The photographs they take must fill hundreds of albums when they go back home!

Once, however, national distinctions struck one immediately, in the food, in the clothes. Now a great sameness is spreading across the world, from frozen pizzas to the universal cornetto ice-cream. Almost as though it was all one country. Perhaps in the past we have clutched on to the old stereotypes as a form of reassurance. It could be, in 30 years' time, national characteristics will have vanished altogether, on holiday and at home! And we'll end up being just one big nation. But how boring that would be!

2C Mind over matter

1.0 and 1.1 page 34

Contrary to what you might imagine, places, prehistoric periods and people can all be remembered easily by sentences made up from a list of initial letters.

The word 'mnemonic' has a simple definition: it's a phrase, verse or saying designed to help you remember something. It comes from the Greek for 'mindful', and it's the only word in the dictionary to begin with *mn*.

I remember my grandfather telling me that 'Richard Of York Gained Battles In Vain' was an easy way to remember the spectrum of colours in a rainbow, (red, orange, yellow, green, blue, indigo and violet).

A good mnemonic can provide a basic structure for learning, and concepts and reasons can be fitted around it.

North America, for example, is a continent most people are familiar with. Even so, few people can remember which Great Lake is which. Try (west to east): 'Super Man Helps Every One' – for lakes Superior, Michigan, Huron, Erie and Ontario.

And if you CAN'T remember which US states border Mexico, just remember C-A-N-T for California, Arizona, New Mexico and Texas. You can groan at the joke if you wish, but you'll never forget the order!

For the US states bordering Canada try this: 'Well, I Must Not Mislead' for Washington, Idaho, Montana, North Dakota, and Minnesota! In fact, the slogan is a good motto for all mnemonic-makers.

South America's more straightforward. Many people already know that 'Colombia's in the Corner, while Ecuador's on the Equator . . . and the only two states without a coastline are Bolivia and Paraguay – and you could use more British Petroleum to get there!

If you've followed the argument so far, you'll be full of mnemonics. They're better 'little and often' than in a big group, and they can be applied to any subject.

But in planning new mnemonics, try to use a strong rhythm – 'Richard Of York Gained Battles In Vain' has lasted because it flows well and it's got a strong rhythm. Try to find memorable but mad logic. A good mnemonic makes learning more enjoyable and much less forgettable!

2.0 page 35

I=interviewer, **D**=Deborah Tannen

I In her first book *You Just Don't Understand*, Deborah Tannen concentrates on the differences between male and female styles of conversation. In her follow-up *That's Not What I Mean!*, she reminds us that we don't have to look to our nearest and dearest for communication failure. Deborah, would you care to elaborate on this?

D Certainly, for example, friends can mistake concern for condescension, and people you meet at parties, for example, can find your questioning offensive. Women in business situations can appear vague because they haven't adopted the brisk question-and-answer style developed by men, just as men can seem distant because they don't realize that women expect the occasional show of human interest. It's all a matter of conversational style.

I Can you give us any more examples . . . ?

D Er, well, there are so many . . . Erm, Americans, for example, like to get a fix on a person's first name, which isn't popular with the British, while Americans who aren't asked questions about themselves by a British person may assume they're downright unfriendly.

I So what advice would you give us . . . ?

D Certainly, the best thing you can do is to stand back and listen. A tape recording is probably one of the best ways to understand your own verbal style.

3.0 page 35

Although it seems that men and women grow up in the same world, how they use language – in different ways and for different purposes – makes it seem that the two sexes are talking at cross-purposes. For women, talk is the glue that holds relationships together; it creates connections between people and a sense of community.

For men, activities hold relationships together; talk is used to negotiate their position in a group and preserve independence. With all these divergent concerns women and men typically talk differently when they are trying to achieve the same end. And they often walk away from the conversation having 'heard' very different interactions.

Consider these two typical examples of confusion:

A woman who owned a cake shop asked her male manager to do something, and he agreed to do it. Days later it hadn't been done. Here's what the woman said: 'The book-keeper needs help with the invoicing. What do you think about helping her out?'

The man had said, 'OK', by which he meant, 'OK, I'll think about helping her out.' He had thought about it and decided that he couldn't spare the time. The owner was upset; she felt she'd, well, given him specific instructions. But what he had heard was a suggestion – one he thought he was free to reject.

Let's take another case. A woman asked her adult son, who lived with her, for help with expenses after he began to work full-time. Weeks later he was acting as if they hadn't spoken about it.

The woman had asked her son for rent money like this: 'I think it would be fair for you to pay rent now.' He replied, 'I'm leaving soon anyway.' The woman walked away from the conversation feeling greatly relieved. But as time passed and no rent appeared, her anger erupted. In the ensuing quarrel it emerged that her son had heard her statement as an opinion, not a request for rent. He had walked away from their initial conversation feeling that the idea of his paying rent had been raised but not settled.

Research by psychologists, sociologists and anthropologists shows that one of the most striking differences between girls' and boys' styles is how they ask – or direct – others to do what they want. At all ages girls are more likely to phrase their preferences as suggestions, appearing to give others options in deciding what to do, while boys tend to give each other commands.

3.2 page 36

So, given these differences, how should the cake shop owner give orders to male employees? She probably wouldn't feel comfortable saying, 'Help the book-keeper with the invoicing today.' A possible solution might be to find a compromise between her indirect style and the more direct style that's typical of men. She might say, 'Sally needs help with the invoicing. I'd like you to help her out today. Is there any reason you can't?'

The 'I'd like you to' should satisfy her sense of politeness, and she's stating the reason for her request. She's also giving him an opportunity to express his reason for not complying, if there is any. But, still it's clear that she's telling him what to do.

Authority relations are also important in the conversation between the mother and her adult son. The mother felt that as the parent and the owner of the house, all she had to do was make her wishes known and her son would automatically feel obliged to honour them. But if she knew that men often *honestly* misinterpret indirect requests, she might've tried to end the conversation with her son by seeking a commitment to act. She may not've been comfortable giving an order like, 'Have a cheque ready for me on Monday,' but she might've asked, 'When can I expect a cheque?' This is polite in the sense of giving him an option, but it's also explicit about what she expects him to do.

Exam practice page 37

S=Susan, **D**=Dave

S But you see, you haven't really thought through the implications of all this. Another way that men's and women's styles differ is that well, most women mix business and personal conversation.

D You mean like talking about the weather?

S No, no, no, no, nothing as mundane as that. Although most British people are quite content to talk about nothing else! No, what I mean is that women will talk about things that really affect them – er, their hopes, fears, troubles . . . They feel that personal conversation establishes the comfortable relationships between them that, well, I suppose, provide the basis for working together; that's what makes it possible for them to conduct their business successfully and efficiently.

D So, what advice would you give, for example, to a woman who works in a male-dominated environment. Or one where males are in the majority?

S I think that a woman who works with men just may have to – how shall I put it? – sort of moderate her desire for this kind of conversation in a work setting, perhaps even tone down the amount of 'personal' small talk.

D And what about a woman who works with other women?

S Ah, well, now that's different! She might not have the option of giving up!

D But are there any concrete examples? Could you give me a genuine instance where you can see this kind of thing in action?

S Er . . . yes. I can think of one case of a woman editor who was employed as the editor of a newsletter. Well, she had so much to do that she decided to run the office as she'd seen men run offices she'd worked in: you know, no time for small talk, get right down to business.

D Sounds as if she meant business! The thing is, did she succeed? And if she didn't, why not?

S Er, well, hang on a minute and you'll find out! She'd only been in the job a short time, when she began to hear rumblings that the women in the office were unhappy with her. They felt she was cold and aloof, that power had gone to her head and made her arrogant.

D So? What did she do about it?

S Well, she decided to modify her style with a compromise between men's and women's styles, allowing some time to chat to people and exchange pleasantries, and this was extremely successful.

D And what about men? Where do they figure in all this great philosophy of yours?

S Ah well, the trouble is, you see, many men resent personal questions! They regard them as an intrusion of their privacy, and may even misinterpret them as an indication of romantic interest!

D So, basically, it's a no-win situation!

S No, I wouldn't say it's as bad as all that. It's just a question of showing moderation – not indulging in too much of any kind of talk in a work situation. I'm not suggesting that we should segregate the sexes! That would be an extremely retrogressive step!

2D Today's technology

1.2 page 39

I=Interviewer, **S1–9**=Speakers 1–9

I In our survey on video games we asked youngsters three questions; firstly, how they felt about paying for video games. 27% replied along these lines:

S1 To tell the truth, I feel as if the manufacturers are ripping me off.

I 20% said:

S2 I feel as if the retailers are overcharging me.

I 27% gave this reply:

S3 To be perfectly honest I think what they charge is more or less fair.

I and a mere 4% admitted:

S4 Actually, I don't think they're expensive – in fact some of them are cheap.

I We then asked whether the price of these games had put them off the console or system that they owned. 28% said:

S5 Not at all!

I and 18% said:

S6 Not really!

I 17% replied:

S7 I would certainly say that I'm not as keen as I was.

I The last question we asked was how long, on average, they played a game before it got boring. 19% said:

S8 I'd say anything from four to six weeks.

I and 14% said:

S9 Certainly never more than two weeks.

2.0 and 2.1 page 39

1 OK, video games might be a cheap form of entertainment, but I certainly don't want my children playing them for hours on end!

2 Many of our younger patients wear a patch over one eye when they play these games. You see there's a very real danger of suffering from what we call 'photosensitive epilepsy'.

3 I can't stop playing once I start a game.

4 I like inviting my friends round to play the games.

5 Every year some of the products become obsolete and we have to order replacements.

6 I think young people are being ripped off by these games and I just won't have them in our house.

7 We feel that our games not only help children to use computers, they also fuel the imagination.

8 The medical research we've been carrying out shows that compulsive players rapidly begin to suffer from a lack of communication skills.

9 I just bought this fantastic game – it's really exciting!

2.2 page 40

P=Presenter, **Ne**=Neil, **Ni**=Nicholas

P When eight-year-old Neill Moore returns home from school, the first thing he wants to do is play with his *Super Nintendo*. Like millions of youngsters, he was given the game as a present and the *Nintendo* console is permanently strapped to the TV set in the family home.
Before Neill can play with his *Nintendo*, he has to complete his homework. The amount of time he spends playing is strictly monitored by his mother.

Ne Well, sometimes my mum won't let me play but I play a lot more during the weekends. At times, I play for up to five hours – especially if my dad's alone with me in the house! I don't think playing the game has made me violent, though. The games aren't bad for you 'cause they help you learn things and they're fun.

P According to the few surveys conducted in the US and Britain, boys are more likely to play video games than girls. Khim Karaud, for example, doesn't play every day and, when she does, the maximum time her mother allows her is half an hour. Nicholas Scott, 11, owns a Sega Mega Drive, which he bought for himself.

Ni Some of the games show you violent moves which you can practise on your friends. I don't find myself becoming aggressive but some of my friends do. They start fighting and they think they're in the video game. I don't own any aggressive games like that but I sometimes borrow them.

2.3 page 40

P=Presenter, **Ne**=Neill, **K**=Khim, **J**=Jaspal, **Ni**=Nicholas

P When eight-year-old Neill Moore returns home from school, the first thing he wants to do is play with his Super Nintendo. Like millions of youngsters, he was given the game as a present and the Nintendo console is permanently strapped to the TV set in the family home.

Ne I like playing Nintendo because I like the characters and the action. My favourite game is Street Fighter 2. I'd like to play all the time but I have to ask my mum and dad before I can play.

P Before Neill can play with his Nintendo, he has to complete his homework. The amount of time he spends playing is strictly monitored by his mother.

Ne Well, sometimes my mum won't let me play but I play a lot more during the weekends. At times, I play for up to five hours – especially if my dad's alone with me in the house! I don't think playing the game has made me violent, though. The games aren't bad for you 'cause they help you learn things and they're fun.

P According to the few surveys conducted in the US and Britain, boys are more likely to play video games than girls. Khim Karaud, for example, doesn't play every day and, when she does, the maximum time her mother allows her is half an hour.

Tapescripts • Module 3A

K I'm not all that keen on playing with it because I think some of the games are boring. They're all about fighting, and after a while it's easy to play them and get a high score. I only wanted a Nintendo 'cause I felt left out. Sometimes I'd rather just be with my friends.

P According to a book by Eugene F Provenzo called *Video Kids*, video games encourage sexism, violence and racism in children. Thirteen-year-old Jaspal Bhatti disagrees.

J I don't think that's right. They're just games, they're exciting. I don't think anyone believes that they are true to life. I like playing them because they're better than watching telly.

P Nicholas Scott, eleven, owns a Sega Mega Drive, which he bought for himself.

Ni I play my Sega because I get bored at home and I like to entertain myself. I'd like to play more during the week but my mum controls the time I can play. She doesn't really like my Sega machine. She hates the noise it makes.

P Nicholas admits that playing the games sometimes distracts him from his homework.

Ni Sometimes I come home and start playing. I leave my homework too late and then I don't feel like doing it. Some of the games show you violent moves which you can practise on your friends. I don't find myself becoming aggressive but some of my friends do. They start fighting and they think they're in the video game. I don't own any aggressive games like that but I sometimes borrow them.

3.1 page 42

1 Do you own any of the following? Tick any which apply.
2 How often in the past six months have you turned down a social engagement because it clashed with a favourite television programme?
3 If you come across an electrical shop with TV sets switched on in the window, what do you do?
4 What do you think about late night educational programmes?
5 Would you give up watching TV for the rest of your life for £100,000?
6 What do you do if your television set ceases to function?
7 Which of these statements do you identify most with?
8 What do you commonly do with one eye on the television? Tick any which apply.

Exam practice page 42

1 You just wouldn't believe how many young people come to me with hearing problems. Very often it's something to do with volume control – you see they walk around everywhere with these headphones, trying to shut themselves off from the rest of the world! They're just asking for trouble really in later life! It can do more damage than loud disco music!
2 We order masses of these every week. The kids get their pocket money and then head for the store. Mind you, they're not new! They're all second-hand – and dirt cheap!, so the kids end up swapping them with their friends. Why spend money going out to see something when a few months later you can see it in your own living room any time you like at the press of a button?
3 The kids are all music fanatics. But when this new digital thing first presented itself we were all a bit sceptical in the staff room at first. Didn't really believe you could recreate the sound of a full orchestra in a music room . . . and with one small round object! But when we heard the reproduction we were absolutely amazed. We immediately got rid of our cassette players and rushed out to equip ourselves with the latest in sound technology!
4 Well, I see a lot of problem families in my line of work and one of the difficulties we notice is that the centre of family life doesn't exist without the box. The thing's never switched off and the whole family sits glued to the thing, and nobody really talks to each other any more. Nobody communicates! And when there is conversation it's usually an argument about who's going to watch what!
5 I started the habit last year when I was revising for my first set of exams. What I really needed was a little background music, nothing too heavy, but then I realized that there were other things worth switching on for, too. I'd never been one for soap opera, or anything else on the TV, for that matter, but it's different with no visual images – when you've got to imagine the setting and characters yourself. I wouldn't be without it now!

3 SPEAKING

3A What if . . . ?

3.0 page 45

And now to this Saturday's programmes. The final historical reconstruction offered in *What if . . . ?* is on Radio 4 on Saturday at 4 p.m. and is unquestionably the most chilling of the series. Military historian Lawrence Freedman and his Russian counterpart Anton Suirkov tell chairman Christopher Andrew what they think would have happened had the 1962 Cuban missile crisis teetered over the edge. Their apocalyptic vision would have been launched had the US actually carried out its threat to bomb the Soviet missile sites. The most alarming disclosure is that the Soviet nuclear capability was actually far greater than Washington calculated and that the subsequent retaliation really could have been fatal.
Immediately after this programme, at 5.40, Martin Wainwright's unrivalled ability . . .

4.1 page 46

The 21st century is hardly light years away. Have you thought where you will be celebrating the new millenium? With a sizeable cash lump sum, payable in the year 2010, to spend as you choose, there's no earthly reason why you shouldn't be celebrating in style, however and wherever you like. All you have to do is invest some of your savings in our very generous scheme!
And just look at these wonderful offers: when you apply for a quotation, you'll receive, completely free and with no obligation whatsoever, a travel alarm clock; once you start your plan a free telephone answering machine will be yours; and finally, if you save £25 a month, you'll get free weekend accommodation for two at a hotel of your choice! All you pay for is breakfast and evening meals.
Cash Escalator from Sun Alliance is a with-profits savings plan with built-in guarantees and bonuses dependent on future profits. The plan also provides life cover and has automatically increasing contributions which we promise will help keep you ahead of inflation.
Phone us now – free of charge – on 0800 525575 extension 335 to see how sizeable your cash sum could be. Lines are open weekdays from 9 a.m. to 8 p.m.
Once accepted, we'll send you full details of the plan.

3B Yesterday and today

2.1 page 51

The subject of our round-the-coastline series of summer programmes tonight is that 'jewel of the south coast', Brighton. Well, you may or may not be aware of it, but Brighton 'invented the seaside'.
It happened in 1753, when a certain Dr Richard Russell explained, in a now historic – and somewhat dubious – publication, the advantages of sea water. The doctor advised his patients not only to immerse themselves in the chilly water, but to drink a pint of it to cure various illnesses that might be troubling them!
With today's high pollution count off many beaches, he might now advise 'taking the waters' in moderation!
Queen Victoria couldn't stand Brighton. The sight of so many people milling round her home, the Royal Pavilion, persuaded her to sell Europe's most exotic seaside palace in 1850. However, Brighton today remains a magnet to all from afar who see the town as one great palace of fun!

3.2 page 54

1 I've been here since breakfast . . . came specially to see it all as it disappears over the cliff! It's better than a film, isn't it? A real thrill!
2 It's impossible to say with any accuracy exactly how long the building will remain standing. It defies all engineering odds – it just shouldn't be here now – there's just no logic behind it at all.
3 We're numb. It's just a nightmare. We've run the place for the last ten years and we just don't know where we go from here – we just don't know what's going to happen now.
4 Yes, we've been selling 'Disaster Strikes' T-shirts at £9.50 each. I suppose some people could call it a bit mercenary. But if anyone

had been killed or injured we wouldn't have done it. It's harmless, and it's good business!
5 I've still got all my wedding photos from the reception we had there a few weeks ago – only a few yards from where the place has just – literally – fallen into the sea! Lucky, eh?

3C/D Art and culture

1.1 page 58

And tonight we have the latest news for you from the world of music. An extract from 'Lifeforms' – 90 minutes of organic soundscapes redefining electronic music in a modern classical atmosphere. Available on CD and cassette from a good music shop near you.

4.1 page 64

R=Reporter, **C**=Commissaire-principal Jean-Claude Rolin

R A castle in rural France was home to Mr and Mrs Van Den Bergen, a gaggle of geese and 1,000 forged masterpieces – until the police burst in and exposed the biggest art scandal in 20 years.
Commissaire-principal Jean-Claude Rolin has no doubt about the importance of the loot.
C This is the biggest art scandal of its type for at least 20 years. The pictures not only look like originals, they have certificates of authenticity. Forged, of course.
R And how did you come to discover this gigantic fraud operation?
C Well, em, I'm no art collector – but I've learnt more about painting in the last few days than I did in all my life! When I get permission, I'll put on an exhibition for the press. I'll let you take photos then. After the trial, the pictures will have to be destroyed. Sad, isn't it?
R But what if they'd been real? What about their market value then?
C Well, the Germans have suggested 500,000 marks, but that's only a reserve price.
R So it could well have been . . .
C . . . a lot more . . .
R But . . . how did you come to discover . . .
C Ah, yes, well it all began with a fateful springtime tour of Germany. You see Mr Van Den Bergen started selling paintings and certificates of authenticity to galleries and auction houses in major German cities like Bonn, Cologne and so on. I'm not allowed to tell you what made them suspicious but the Germans told us the seller was using postal addresses in Orleans, which is why the inquiry is based here. There were other addresses in Paris but these were just post-boxes where he could collect letters or have them forwarded. A few months ago the whole business would have taken ages to clear up, but new European police co-operation meant that our German detective was able to operate with us in a few hours and Van Den Bergen was apprehended by the police in Germany.
R And how have the local people taken all this?
C Well, the local people didn't see him very often. He was occasionally spotted riding through the countryside on his bicycle . . . but he was obviously much too busy working on his forger's . . . er, on his assembly line! . . . and typing out certificates of authenticity!
R Under French law, the maximum sentence for forging artworks is only five years in jail, and he won't serve more than three if he's well-behaved. So while there may be hundreds of anxious collectors taking another look at the masterpiece on the mantelpiece, the worst punishment Mr Van Den Bergen could receive could be the governor's eventual refusal of an urgent request for brushes, canvas and an easel!

4 LISTENING

4A Achievements

1.0 page 66

1 Without a doubt the best thing ever invented was the electric iron. I remember my grandmother standing for hours warming irons in the fire then lifting the red hot things to press her linen tablecloths!
2 No doubt about it – the electric light bulb. It revolutionized our whole existence. Led the way to all sorts of improvements in the quality of life.
3 I would say the sewing machine. I mean, I've read all about girls sewing by candlelight and ruining their eyesight doing jobs that can be done in seconds with a machine.
4 I reckon the pocket watch was the greatest thing ever invented. Definitely! How could anybody have been on time before it well . . . arrived on the scene?

1.1 page 66

As you may or may not know, Joseph Swan was born in the north of England in 1828. He left school at 13 and began working as an apprentice in a chemist's shop before moving to Newcastle in 1846 where he joined White's, the firm of his future brother-in-law, as a qualified chemist. Photographic plates were also manufactured by the company and Swan soon developed a keen interest in these. This led to his development of a production process for dry photographic plates and in 1862, he succeeded in patenting a commercial process for carbon printing.
In the same year, he got married to Frances White. But she was to die six years later, and in 1871 her sister Hannah became his wife. He was the father of seven children.
Meanwhile, Swan's work moved on to the study of light and electricity and, before a fascinated audience of 700 in Newcastle in 1879, he demonstrated his invention, the first electric bulb.
The Swan Electric Lamp Company was formed in 1881, and in 1883 Swan joined with Thomas Edison, who'd obtained the patent for a carbon filament lamp. Swan's improvements to Edison's design proved a huge success.
By the time he died in 1914, Swan had received many honours, including a knighthood in 1904. He will, however, always be remembered as the man who invented the first efficient method for turning electrical energy into light.

2.0 page 67

Have you noticed how many conventional book prizes tend to overlook the kind of books you enjoy reading yourself? Wouldn't it be great if juries simply recommended the most entertaining read of the year? Well, the *Thumping Good Read Award* sets out to do precisely that.
To get on the shortlist, a book has to be a 'gripping novel with real page-turning quality'. Even more crucially, the judges who select the winner are not literary professionals, but members of the public – people who read exclusively for pleasure.
Later this year we will announce this year's prize-winner. In the meantime, why not follow the example of our panel and read all six shortlisted titles? On the programme today, we're going to talk about two of them. The others will appear in next week's programme . . .

2.1 page 68

First of all, *A Simple Plan* by Scott Smith. Beating their way through a snowdrift, Hank and Jacob Mitchell, and their low-life friend Lou, stumble upon the wreckage of an aircraft. In the cockpit is a dead pilot and behind him is a duffel bag containing over $4 million. Against Hank's better instincts, they concoct a 'foolproof' plan to keep the money. But when mistrust sets in, the quiet Hank descends into a spiral of betrayal and murder. Robert Harris, who knows what it takes to win the Thumping Good Read Award, describes the book as a 'work of art'. According to Robert, it's 'original and beautifully written'.

And the next book is *Night Shall Overtake Us* by Kate Saunders.
Four Edwardian schoolgirls swear a blood vow of eternal friendship. But, as they innocently share their dreams of romance, none has yet foreseen the nightmare of the Great War, which will turn their world upside down. Each girl experiences a loss of innocence, starting with Aurora – a fiery Irish redhead who becomes a suffragette, campaigning for the right of women to vote, then finds her calling as a nurse in the trenches. But, in this saga, offering a heady mixture of heroism, tragedy and unrestrained passion, who will break the solemn vow first? This novel is a triumph on all fronts!

3.1 page 68

On our programme this afternoon we welcome Sam Gray.
Now, Sam used to be a top male model but now, with the publication of his novel *EGO*, he's well on his way to becoming a top writer too. And, we can assure you, he's more than just a handsome face!

Tapescripts • Module 4A

3.2 page 69

I=Interviewer, **S**=Sam

I At only 27, this Cambridge graduate has been to the very heights of the modelling profession, but now his sights are set firmly on a successful career as a novelist.
He's not exactly starting on the ground floor, either. Not for Sam the suspense of sending in an unsolicited manuscript and waiting around for rejection. *EGO*, his first novel was snapped up straight away. In addition to that, he's handsome, erudite and has experience of top modelling around the globe, so it would be easy to be envious of his luck. But despite all his good living, Sam's own ego is mercifully small and his self-deprecation is endearing and funny.
Sam, welcome to the studio.

S Thanks, it's a pleasure to be invited . . . and thanks for that great intro. But I was well, lucky, I suppose. I went straight to the top of the modelling tree without ever doing any of the rotten jobs, and here I am now with a published novel at the first attempt.

I And what made you quit the world of modelling?

S Well, I suppose the real truth of the matter is that with my hair falling out and my English-tea-stained teeth, things were looking rather dicey.

I So what's your novel about?

S Well, it's called *EGO* and I regard it as my saviour, it saved me from a possible future of smaller parts and dwindling fees, and it's an everyday story of modelling folk. Their trials and tribulations, their ups and downs. I'm not knocking the modelling world – it was very good to me. But, you know, it's a bit of a vacuous profession. Still, you only need to work one day in 14 to have a comfortable life style . . . and you travel the world first class!

I And you're still way up there above the rest of us poor mortals! I know you're off to a very high-powered function in a little while. And I hear you've even got contacts in the White House! Are you going to make what you're learning from them the subject of your next novel?

S Can't say at the moment, I'm afraid.

I Well, If it's as gripping as your first, I'm convinced that you've got a handsome career in front of you. Thank you for coming, Sam.

S Thank you.

3.3 page 69

The inappropriate word is in *italics*

1 At only 27, this Cambridge graduate, has been to the very *highs* of the modelling profession.
2 But now his *sighs* are set firmly on a successful career as a novelist.
3 *EGO*, his first novel was *snipped* up straight away.
4 In addition to that, he's handsome, erudite and has experience of top modelling around the *grove*.
5 But *in spite* all his good living, Sam's own ego is mercifully small and his self-deprecation is endearing and funny.
6 Well, I suppose the real truth of the matter is that with my hair falling out and my English-tea-*strained* teeth, things were looking rather dicey.
7 I'm not knocking the modelling *word* – it was very good to me.
8 And you're still way up there above the rest of us poor *morals*!
9 And I hear you've even got *contracts* in the White House.
10 Well, if it's as gripping as your first, I'm convinced you've got a handsome *carrier* in front of you.

4.0 page 69

P=Presenter, **L**=Listener

P Good evening ladies and gentlemen and welcome to another edition of *The Power of The Press*. Since our last programme our researchers have been out and about investigating questions sent in by you, the listeners. The first tonight comes from a lady in the Midlands.

L Has the course of events ever been changed significantly as a result of a letter written to, or published by, a national newspaper?

P Peter Rainer reports . . .

4.1 page 70

R=Peter Rainer, **A**='Lady Allen'

R We did, indeed, come up with an answer to this one. Apparently on July the 15th, 1944, *The Times* published a letter from a certain Lady Allen of Hurtwood. This letter described the conditions suffered by many children who were living in local authority institutional care, or who were being looked after by voluntary agencies which were, and I quote 'repressive . . . generations out of date and unworthy of our traditional care of children.'
She went on to say

A 'Many who are orphaned, destitute or neglected rely totally on charity to support them and are despised by those more fortunate than themselves.'

R She criticised having staff who were

A 'for the most part overworked, underpaid and untrained.'

R She also criticised the lack of recognised training and adequate inspection and supervision. She ended up by calling for a public enquiry.
A stream of letters followed in her support. In fact, the editor of *The Times* twice tried to bring the correspondence to an end. The number of letters the newspaper had received was greater than for any other issue ever dealt with in the 'letters' column of the newspaper.
Six months later, Lady Allen made her case again in a pamphlet *Whose Children?* A few days after its publication, the campaign attracted more interest because of the inquest into the death of 13-year-old Denis O'Neill. Denis had died at the hands of the very man who was supposed to be acting as his 'father'. He had been sent by his local authority to live with a family on a remote sheep farm in the countryside and, after the tragedy, his death was widely reported in the press.
All this agitation – largely prompted by that first letter – was responsible for the government establishing a committee in 1945, to investigate the care of children 'deprived of normal home life with their own families and relatives.'
It reported in 1946 and led directly to the creation of children's departments. These departments, certainly until they were taken over by the new social services departments in 1971, completely transformed for the better the face of official child care in this country.

Exam practice page 70

P=Presenter, **B**=Bill Brown

P Whether it's French, German, Italian or Spanish that the crew are learning, the formula is the same. Forget any image that might remain of classroom techniques, of hours of weary repetition, and grammar learnt from books with improbable phrases. Here Nation Airline cabin crew are learning their new languages the very best way possible, from life in lifelike situations. The training centre is based on acquiring a living, breathing, useful grasp of a language in the most natural way possible, by hearing it and using it every day in surroundings that are informative, relaxed and lend themselves to creating anything from a mock-up of an aircraft cabin to a table in a restaurant. In the past cabin staff were not particularly noted for their linguistic talents but things have changed drastically. Not only are there more foreign language speakers within the airline than ever before, but the numbers are increasing week by week, thanks to the enthusiasm of the crews and the talent of the language trainers.
Bill Brown, who manages the language unit, is proud of what has been accomplished in the six years he has been in the job.

B Our principal objective is to teach our shorthaul crews, but we also have longhaul crews who are anxious to improve their skills and we fit them in as and when we can. Language training's become so popular that we have to juggle our way through ever-lengthening waiting lists. However, just occasionally we have specific needs to increase the number of speakers of a particular language. It's something we take very seriously and a lot of thought has gone into the best way of handling it. We've come up with a wonderful idea called 'Tasterdays'. These are exactly what they say: just a day and just a taste of what it's like to be an airline language student. Tasterdays are compulsory for some crews but they've already proved irresistible!

P So, let's have a closer look at what one of these days entails . . .

4B Survival

1.1 page 71

1 In this country anything on four wheels is still an untackled problem – and a political hot potato! Too hot to handle! The government's admitted it can't build enough roads to accommodate all the vehicles people will acquire in the future but has no ideas how to, er . . . to, er . . . deal with the situation. So what's happened? As a result the budget for building new roads has quite simply been trimmed down. I mean to say – it's a question of no action – no solutions!

2 The only way to avoid global warming is for the rich world to set an example by cutting fossil fuel use by, well, I would say reducing it by at least 80%. Developers, designers and planners don't display much understanding of the nature of the problem. Maybe they don't want to understand! It wouldn't take a great change to suggest that, say, erm, a new building should be put up only if it could show its impact on the environment – positive rather than negative, of course. Then it would be allowed.

3 The environmental crisis tells us that human societies, particularly those in the so-called developed world, have undervalued the environment – just not appreciated it, if you like. They've put material consumption before environmental integrity – and we're running out of time! The timescale for action is definitely shortening. There's no doubt about it! Twenty years ago environmental disaster was predicted in 100 years' time. Last year we were given 20 years to get our act together!

2.0 page 72

So, if you're feeling tense, this morning we're going to do something about it! Finding a therapy that suits your temperament, lifestyle and budget needs careful planning! Above all, stress relief should be a treat, so choose something you'll enjoy!
First of all aerobic exercise: its role in stress relief is to release nature's tranquillizers into your system creating a feeling of well-being. You'll probably feel, sleep and look better. You should aim for at least 15 minutes of aerobic exercise three times each week and you'll notice an improvement in how you feel, sleep and look!
Next, the Alexander Technique, which is a system of re-educating your breathing and posture. You'll learn how to fall into a natural, easy way of moving. It's extremely useful when mental and physical symptoms are closely connected. Symptoms which have this mental and physical interdependence are, for example, asthma, stammering, insomnia and headaches. Relaxation tapes lead you through a series of muscle relaxing and breathing exercises. Clinical psychologists often prescribe these for very anxious patients. They can be used as often as three times a day for the first week. However anxious they are, patients find that the exercises reduce everyday stress.
And last but not least, Yoga, that ancient discipline of mental and physical exercise, which is based on moving or static postures and stretches, some of which are admittedly rather complicated. But don't be put off by these seemingly complicated postures – even easy sitting and lying postures are immensely beneficial!

2.1 page 72

A
Well, we thought we'd investigate these Stressbusters a little more thoroughly – so we've produced a list of pros and cons for you. First: the pros.
As far as aerobic exercise is concerned, the pros are easy to identify: it's extremely easy to set up and you'll find that it really does keep you fit. With the Alexander Technique, one-to-one sessions give you the chance to deal with your particular individual problems, such as feeling nervous, or insomnia. You should benefit in several different ways – actors and singers, for instance, use it to improve voice delivery – and it's great if you've got a bad back or suffer from pains in your shoulders.
Relaxation tapes couldn't be easier to use. They're instantly available and, of course, not at all expensive! You don't need any special sort of kit, just a tape recorder, which most of us have anyway!
With Yoga, you can start at any age, and you don't have to do it well to feel the benefits. There's no one-upmanship in classes, and all you need is loose, stretchy clothing.

B
And now, for the cons. As with everything, there's, there's usually a downside!
Aerobic exercise carries a fairly high risk of hurting yourself. If you're over 25, or have any back or joint problems, find a qualified instructor. And, although the exercise is usually an excellent balance for emotional or mental pressures, it's also a stress in itself. If you really need to slow down, the extra effort may make you over-tired. So, if you don't feel better, try something more gentle.
Unfortunately, with the Alexander Technique the initial outlay is high – you'll need a course of at least 10–15 lessons. But it's a lifetime's investment – afterwards you'll only require one or two sessions a year. Also, it won't be until around the fifth lesson that you'll begin to feel better, so it's not an immediate way of unlocking tension.
The trouble with relaxation tapes is that it can be difficult to get your family to take you seriously and leave you alone. Boredom can easily set in, so it's often better to, to find some, er, different music to exercise to. And, oh, by the way, you should never use a tape when driving!
You may find it difficult to fit Yoga into your daily life pattern. You, you must find a class, as books and videos are only useful as a back-up. If you're an er, er, get-up-and-go person, you may find it too quiet and inward-looking.

2.2 page 73

1 therapy
2 temperament
3 budget
4 tranquillizers
5 muscle
6 psychologists
7 ancient
8 beneficial
9 loose
10 stretchy

3.0 page 73

You know what they say: if you come face to face with a North American mountain lion, don't run away. Attack! They are as powerful as jaguars and have teeth as long as your little finger but, if you attack them, they are basically respectful, non-aggressive creatures!
They're also highly persecuted – or have been. For years, they've been shot at by ranchers and hunters. Lion numbers have levelled off recently but US state game agencies still know too little about them – certainly not enough to ensure their survival in the face of expanding human numbers.
If you're interested, the most direct way to find out about the lions, is to join one of the many expeditions organized by *Earthwatch*. Since 1972, *Earthwatch* has been organizing and supporting scientific expeditions and projects with the aim of 'improving understanding of the planet, the diversity of its inhabitants, and the processes that affect what they call 'the quality of life on earth'.
Understanding what affects this 'quality of life' can be translated into the sharp end of eco-tourism – a logical step for anyone tired of familiar itineraries and package deals strung together by commercial tour companies. *Earthwatch* is anything but a commercial tour company. It organizes trips to the Albion Mountains. Five expeditions to the Albion Mountains are planned for this year at a cost of about $1,300 dollars per person, which covers food and accommodation. According to *Earthwatch* these are real expeditions not tours! To join these expeditions you have to be a member of *Earthwatch* but they have special membership rates for families. You can obtain further information by writing to *Earthwatch*.

4.0 page 74

Good afternoon, ladies and gentlemen and welcome to the Sealed Knot Society's re-enactment of the final battle of the civil war fought between rival groups in this country. The battle took place in this very area 350 years ago today, and led to the parliamentary system that we still have nowadays.
Today's re-enactment of the civil war battle promises to be one of the biggest and most spectacular events the Society has ever staged, and, around the arena, you'll find a children's funfair, refreshment stalls, music and much more . . .
The members of the Society, all in 17th century costumes, are coming onto the field at this very moment, if you can see them there. It's easy to imagine, looking at the costumes the participants are wearing, what the scene might have looked like all those years ago.
You'll probably notice rather a lot of women in the line-up – of course, in those days women didn't fight, but if a man were going to war, it would be very difficult for his wife to make a living, so she would follow the soldiers in the hope of making a living from her husband's plunder and wages.
From where I'm standing, it seems that the crowd on my left are about 20 deep. Please feel free there to move down to the other end of the

field where there is masses of space – and you'll also get a much better view of the exciting manoeuvres.

Exam practice page 76

Today we find ourselves right in the heart of the country for a performance by the Sealed Knot Battle Re-enactment Society. Just in case you've never heard of it, the Sealed Knot was founded in the 1960s, in 1968 to be exact, by a distinguished soldier and military historian who had carried out extensive research into the civil war itself. Indeed the object of the Society was promoting public interest in, and hence public support for research into, the history of the civil war in this country.

The Society is Europe's largest and most experienced re-enactment society, with over 3,000 enthusiastic members at its disposal. Although participants are all amateurs (there isn't a single professional participant among them), they have a wealth of experience and are capable of putting on a wide range of events. A portion of all fees is allocated to the Society's Charity Fund, which is distributed to different charities on an annual basis. Other profits go towards the Society itself, although participants are not paid, as such. Total charitable contributions are now approaching two million pounds, and many different charities have benefited from the Society's activities. So, if you feel that your event or charity might benefit from the ability of the Society to draw large crowds, please let them know your requirements. They claim to re-enact the past on behalf of the future, or 'bring the past alive in aid of the future' as they put it, and attract the large crowds who'll guarantee that your event is a success. Large crowds mean more money for good causes and the Society will be happy to attend your special event. You only have to ask!

4C A question of gender

1.1 page 76

Let's consider for a moment five essential abilities:
1 awareness of emotions.
2 mathematical ability.
3 verbal skills.
4 thinking in three dimensions.
5 remembering locations.

2.1 page 78

Well, the answer to question one: numbers 1 and 3 were the same.
In our tests 41% of women and 64% of men scored correctly.
The perfect score for question two was 20 and out of that score the average for women was 15 and for men, 12.
For question three: the women beat the men again with 4.1 synonyms per word as against 2.2 for the men. Now I don't know how these results might compare with your own tests but . . .

2.2 page 78

Stuttering affects four times as many girls as boys.
Men are better at thinking in three dimensions.
Men possess an ability to read other people's hidden motives and meanings.
Women are better at remembering apparently unconnected items.
Girls develop a larger vocabulary.
Boys often begin speaking earlier than girls.
Girls catch up with boys when they enter secondary school.

3.1 page 78

Men excel at thinking in three dimensions. This may be due to ancient evolutionary pressures relating to hunting, which requires orientating oneself while pursuing prey.
Women excel at remembering the location of random items, perhaps reflecting evolutionary pressure on women who foraged for their food. Those who go searching for food must recall complex patterns formed of apparently unconnected items.

4.0 page 79

S=Sally, **M**=Martin

M Humans think there's nothing more natural than males and females in mutual pursuit of the urge to be fruitful and multiply. But nature has more than one script! Not every species has two sexes, for example. And even when it does, neither their behaviour nor their origin necessarily conform to human habits! I went along to talk to Sally Davies at the Central Zoo to find out more about the bizarre behaviour of some of the creatures who inhabit the earth.
S Well, one of the more bizarre cases in point is the turtle. Among most reptiles, males are literally made in the shade.
M And how does that come about?
S Er . . . take the gender of a turtle hatchling. It's determined not by chromosomes but by the temperature at which it was incubated. Eggs develop in nests located in sunny areas, where it's warm and toasty, give rise to females.
M So eggs nestled in shady places will yield a crop of males!
S Exactly – and it may be five degrees Centigrade cooler. Now, another bizarre case is the whiptail lizard. For some varieties of these lizards there's no such thing as a battle of the sexes.
M Ah, yes, I remember that one. All of them are female, aren't they?
S Absolutely! But in a somewhat unusual process, they produce eggs that hatch without ever being fertilized. Yet, because they evolved from lizards that come in two sexes, pairs of the single-minded creatures will take turns playfully pretending to be male!
M Now, I think you were going to tell us about an unusual bird next, if I'm not mistaken.
S Uh, hu! The jacana. Yes, female jacana birds usually rule the roost on every shore, marsh and rice field where these long-legged creatures abound. They're generally larger than the males, which are saddled with the duties of building the nest, incubating the eggs and raising the chicks.
M That's the one which . . . I think . . . that in some varieties females regularly jilt their domestic-minded mates and search for other available males, isn't it?
S Absolutely right! And finally, those strange creatures, cichlids.
M Ah yes, aren't those the fish that come in three sexes?
S You have been doing your homework, haven't you? That's right – you can find brightly coloured males, paler females, and feeble males that look and act like females. There are only a few genuine males in a school and, if one of these dies, an ambitious weak male can change its pale colour in an attempt to pretend it's become its rival. If another 'genuine' male appears, however, it can just as quickly revert to its former pale self!
M Well, Sally, thank you for taking us through some of the stranger phenomena . . .

5.0 page 80

1 sensitized
2 bias
3 refrain
4 boost
5 eliminating
6 underscores
7 barred
8 coaching
9 handicap
10 well-funded
11 amplified
12 genes
13 Myra
14 David

Exam practice page 80

M=Mary, **D**=David

M Well, I think teachers may play a larger role than nature in differentiating between the sexes. Studies show that they tend to favour boys by calling on them more often and pushing them harder.
D But surely . . .
M Just a second. Can I finish? Myra and David Sadker, they're professors of education at, actually I can't remember exactly where! – an American university, but can't recall which, sorry! – have found that girls do better when teachers are sensitized to gender bias and refrain from sexist language, like the use of 'man' to mean all of us. Having single-sex classes in maths and science can also boost female performance because it eliminates favouritism and male disapproval of female achievement.
D So if what you're implying is true – and I guess what you're saying is that the success of such simple educational reforms only underscores the basic social issue: given that there may be real innate differences between the sexes, what are we going to do about them? A female advantage in reading emotions could be interpreted to mean that males should be barred from psychiatry – or that they need more coaching. Or a male advantage in math could be used to confine girls to compositions and poetry – or the

decision could be made to compensate by putting more effort into girls' math education. We Americans, in effect, already compensate for boys' apparent handicap in verbal skills by making reading the centrepiece of primary school education. How far down the line do we take this?

M Well, I think I'd have to answer that by saying that we're cultural animals, and these are ultimately cultural decisions. In fact, the whole discussion of innate differences is itself heavily shaped by cultural factors. Why, for example, in the US is the study of innate differences such a well-funded topic right now, which happens to be a time of organized feminist challenge to the ancient sexual division of power? Why do the media tend to get excited when scientists find an area of difference and ignore the many reputable studies that come up with no differences at all?

D If you're implying that however science eventually defines it, the difference can be amplified or minimized by human cultural arrangements: if you're saying that the, the choice is up to us and not our genes then . . . I guess I'd go along with that.

4D Points of view

1.0 page 81

1 Really! (flat then falling intonation)
2 Really! (rising intonation with a slight fall)
3 Really! (rising intonation)

1.1 page 81

1 It's not raining, is it? (rising intonation)
2 We'd better go, hadn't we? (falling intonation)
3 Well, after all, it's not the end of the world, is it? (falling intonation)
4 He can't be serious, can he? (rising intonation)
5 She won't get the job, will she? (rising intonation)
6 You know you'd be better off without him, don't you? (falling intonation)

2.0 page 82

1 As if we didn't have enough coverage – what with the World Cup, endless Olympics and tennis, to name but a few! – we've now got to suffer a series on national sporting passions! Speaking as a totally non-sports person, isn't it about time TV channels woke up and faced the fact that not everybody is interested in several consecutive hours of that kind of thing!

2 May I congratulate you on a truly superb portrait of the biologist Rupert Sheldrake. The programme succeeded in bringing alive the problems of being shunned by the rest of the scientific world, especially when you come up with something like a genetic theory of your own! Many thanks for what I consider to be a fascinating subject – and a really good programme!

3 I just had to ring and say how . . . er . . . well . . . disappointed I was with that series set in Italy. Apart from the fact that it's not my idea of fun watching someone trying to prepare food in the middle of a deserted square in Italy in the pouring rain – I have to admit that it was the soggy ravioli, which must rate as one of the most untempting cookery demonstrations ever, that really put me off!

4 How you can possibly call the trivia that emerged last night at 7.30 a comedy quiz beats me. For one thing, it wasn't funny – and for another – those would-be comedians didn't really answer any of the questions. They were so busy trying to be so funny that the real object of the programme disappeared in a gaggle of forced giggles!

5 Is there any chance of us getting a really accurate forecast? Every night I sit there watching those flashing arrows and fronts moving about all over the place and listening to the hopeful predictions of the weather people, and I've hardly . . . hardly . . . ever been able to rely on it one hundred per cent. You'd think that with all this . . . this new-fangled technology, they'd be a bit more accurate, wouldn't you?

3.0 page 83

1 We interrupt this programme to bring you a gale warning. Last night continuous rain in the west of the country resulted in rivers bursting their banks and widespread damage to property. In some areas local residents have already been evacuated. The Met. Office has just issued a warning of more flooding and severe gales. Anyone threatened by flood waters should contact their emergency services immediately and request help before the gales hit their area.

2 Today, human resources management is an issue that is of great importance to anyone aiming for a senior managerial role. The Sydney Business School has a wealth of experience in both the commercial and public sectors. Should you be interested in applying for a course, or require further information, ring our free phone service, open 24 hours a day, on 246724.

3 The original sirens in classic mythology were women whose song was so lovely, it made passing sailors forget everything else – especially navigation! Certainly, James Dhondi's music for the new opera *The Sirens*, at the Classic theatre, does not aspire to this power. The best advice I could give you would be to buy a good CD and have a night in!

4 Those parents at a loss as to how to survive the school holidays, try a rod and a tin of worms! It keeps the kids occupied for hours on end! Anyone over 12 needs a licence before they can fish in this country but, however old you are, you must find out who owns the stretch of water you intend to visit. You'll need their permission and might have to pay a fee.

5 The best advice new dramatists can be given is to write about the world they know and the characters they have grown up with. Perhaps the greatest skill of Geoff McQueen, who died aged 46, was to create characters that sprang from his personal experience. If you've never seen any of his TV dramas, or if you want to see them again, watch out for tributes in the near future!

4.0 and 4.1 page 84

1 Space technology has aided the development of lightweight, artificial limbs, rechargeable heart pacemakers and lightweight thermal blankets used in mountain rescue. In short, it's given a major boost to a revolution which has seen more progress in my own field of scientific research in the last 50 years than in the previous 2000!

2 There are few sounds as inharmonious in the middle of the night as loud snores from the next pillow. In my own practice I've often treated cases of snoring wrecking marriages and threatening health – particularly where snorers regularly stop breathing and wake themselves and their partner up throughout the night.

3 Just after the turn of the century, a politician was quoted as saying: 'Reading standards are falling because parents no longer read to their children and too much time is spent listening to the gramophone.' Well, the gramophone may be no longer with us, but change the technology and the same could be said by my fellow teachers of pupils today. TV is seen as harmful to the reading health of the nation!

4 I belong to a party whose policy seems to be putting up educational standards through parental involvement . . .but I'm sceptical about the roles of parents. Some obviously take a great interest in their children's education and attend meetings at school and so on, but a great many do not, and would rather go to the pub!

5 There's nothing more annoying in a supermarket than to see an undisciplined child running around causing mayhem, handling cartons and packets without being told off! As well as irresponsible parents, it's the fault of the store managers for tolerating such anti-social behaviour! Shouldn't be allowed.

4.2 page 85

See key on page 151.

Exam practice page 85

1 Erm, I've always been an easy-going sort of person – in my job you've got to be. I can't afford to get too involved with people I've arrested – enforcing the law can be depressing because I usually know who's going to end up doing exactly the same thing time and time again! But I can't let it worry me. I'm usually cheerful and I try to help people whenever I can !

2 I have to admit that on occasions life does get me down. No special reason, really. I've got two lovely kids – twins, actually, and I work part-time on the till at a bank just round the corner. Maybe I try to do too much, then I feel I can't cope, can't seem to get myself involved in well, . . . what I'm doing.

Tapescripts • Task bank 6A

3 Well, I mean, you can't take it seriously, can you? You'd get too depressed! I always try to see the funny side of things. Take my job, for instance. Between you and me, it's not exactly my idea of heaven, driving people round all day long. But you meet all sorts, so it can't be bad, can it?

4 To be honest, I've never been much of a socializer. Never been what you might call 'at ease' in the company of others. That's why I decided to do what I do. Just give me a keyboard and a screen and I'm content - much happier with machines than with other people! And much happier with figures than with words!

5 I've always regarded life as a sort of gift . . . Let's face it, when you look at the kind of world we live in, you've got to be grateful for what you've got! I've worked hard - I know tinkering about with other people's vehicles isn't eveybody's cup of tea. Some people think I'm mad to have such a 'dirty' job! But I love it. It's never been in my nature to wish for anything more!

5 PAPER 5 TASK BANK

There are no tapescripts for Unit 5

6 PAPER 4 TASK BANK

Activities for Part 1

1 Brooklyn Center schools' programs page 96

P=Presenter, **R**=Pete Randal

P In our *Around America* programme this evening we travel to Brooklyn, to hear about the Brooklyn Center for Urban Environment. Pete Randal reports:

R The Brooklyn Center for Urban Environment, or the BCUE, prides itself on its ability to enable you to discover 'urban countryside'.
The BCUE school programs attract over 30,000 children a year, from every school district in Brooklyn, and from all over the city.
The children range in age from pre-kindergarten through high school, and learn to care about the environment by participating in over 30 different programs. Over 70% of these children are of minority origin, and include recent immigrants to America from all over the world.
These unique programs for school classes are infused with local and global environmental content. They incorporate subjects on the curriculum appropriate to each grade level drawn from science, art, architecture, mathematics, language arts and social studies, and cover the broad environmental spectrum between unspoilt nature and the structures of the city.

More than 1,000 teachers annually participate in teacher training and development workshops presented by the Center's education staff. The staff believe that both teachers and students receive the gifts of observation and environmental sensitivity which will last them a lifetime.
In addition to school programs, BCUE adult and family audiences number over 6,000 per year, participating in walking tours, bus and boat trips, workshops and seminars. Each season of events has a theme, such as *East River Waterfront development* or *the imprint of the Military on Brooklyn*.
After-school programs at BCUE provide fun while developing a caring environment foundation. Families with children aged four through 14 years old enrol in environmental and science programs, which include a Summer Day Camp. These after-school programs occur at local schools and parks, and in several disadvantaged areas.

2 High-tech spy page 97

P=Presenter, **R**=Robin Smith, **J**=John Vance

P What's infra-red but green all over? The latest high-tech spy! Robin Smith reports on why the Automobile Club wants police to expose the dirtiest drivers with new 'green' cameras to crack down on pollution in city streets.

R The motoring group has spent two years working on this project, which uses infra-red technology to check exhaust fumes from passing vehicles in the same way video cameras can record licence numbers.
It claims the new technology, which was developed by scientists at Denver University, can identify offenders in less than a third of a second, compared to three minutes for existing video technology.
Yesterday members of the Department of Transport were invited to watch the first in a series of roadside checks using the camera on car emissions.
I talked to John Vance, a spokesperson for the Automobile Club.

J Speed cameras have dramatically reduced accident levels in urban accident spots; and green cameras could prove just as successful in enforcing environmental traffic laws. Well-signposted speed cameras act as a real deterrent, with some sites reporting a 48% decrease in traffic violations. Pollution cameras could provide an, an equally effective deterrent without the need to ban cars from our cities.

R The Automobile Club particularly wants the police to target what it calls the 'gross polluters', that is to say a hard-core 10% of motorists who are actually responsible for more than half the national total of carbon monoxide emissions.
Next month, police and environmental authorities in California, where levels of car ownership are very high, will be testing infra-red remote sensing equipment alongside their freeways, allowing highway patrols to pick up regular offenders for prosecution.

3 Artist's eye page 97

In my teens, while trying to convince myself that I had a talent for art, I remember being pleased to hear that artists with poor colour vision do see and paint the world quite differently.
If, for example, you look at the world through brown-tinted sunglasses, you lose colour discrimination. You can't tell the difference between pale yellow and white, the blues become muddy and you have to paint a very violent blue to see it clearly.
This is a feature of the late paintings of Claude Monet, who had cataracts. Insignificant cataracts affect the majority of us in later life but only in a minority of cases do these become large and dense enough to require treatment. In the type Monet suffered from, the lens becomes brownish rather than opaque. As a result, in the late paintings of his garden at Giverny in France, you can see the whites becoming more yellow and the blues becoming progressively darker. Monet complained at the time that he found his own work increasingly dark and muddy. He even slashed several canvases in despair and – because bright light viewed through a cataract tends to 'scatter', like light through a dirty window, he always avoided painting in direct sunlight.
In a letter to a friend in 1922 Monet wrote, 'my poor eyesight makes me see everything in a complete fog.' Increasingly, he had difficulty recognizing people's faces.
He finally agreed to have cataract surgery in 1923, aged 80, three years before his death from lung disease.

4 Theme park page 98

P=Presenter, **S**=Sally Hoggart

P Theme parks can be heaven or they can be hell. So, as the holiday season starts to rev up, Sally Hoggart offers an insider's guide to getting the most out of Zenith Towers theme park.

S On a busy day, 25,000 people come through the turnstiles. At peak times, it's probable that a majority are standing in queues. As in all big theme parks, waiting your turn is by far the most time-consuming activity! But, if you can reach the car parks by 9 a.m., you can hit all the big rides before the queues really begin to build up!
Your children will probably want to come back if you have time, and, for £5 a head, you can buy a ticket for the following day. But you don't have to decide whether you want to come back at this cheap rate until just before you leave the park.
It's also important to relax! Slow the children down enough to have an hour or so resting and relaxing on a lawn; this will build up vital stamina for the rest of the day.
For those of you looking for something to buy, the gift shop in the Towers itself is marginally less horrific than those outside! There is a first rate and well supervised indoor children's play area, available to persons up to the age of six. Our offspring adored it and you could safely leave yours there for an hour or so while you did grown-up things.

Queues start for the Peter Rabbit ice show an hour before each thrice-daily performance. But the auditorium is so big that you could almost certainly arrive ten minutes before the performance and still get in.

The Haunted House is much too frightening for small children. If yours shows signs of panic there is an escape hatch just before you get to the really scary bit!

Oh, and by the way, if you don't want to carry gifts and souvenirs around with you, you can ask for them to be held for you at the exit.

The rides continue in the rain, unless it's a serious downpour, but queues are shorter. Souvenir plastic ponchos cost £4.50, so bring your own raincoat if the weather looks bad. Rain doesn't make that much difference to attendance, since most people arrange their trips days or weeks in advance.

All in all, Zenith Towers is pretty good. It's not Disney World, but then it doesn't claim to be, and it's a fair bit cheaper. In summer you can stay for 11 hours, which makes it excellent value!

Activities for Part 2

1 City robbery   page 98

Detectives released the first video images yesterday of the two men believed to have been involved in robbing a jeweller's shop in the city seven days ago.

But David Tucker, head of the crime squad, conceded that the video pictures taken a week ago were not very clear. The camera which filmed the men was about 200 metres from where the robbery took place, in fact just 200 metres away from a parked lorry which the robbers later used as a getaway vehicle. The men were also filmed wearing hoods as they ran towards the lorry after the robbery.

The pictures are timed at 8.57 am last Saturday – just half an hour before the robbery occurred. Witnesses have confirmed that at some time during this half-hour, they saw the two men, without hoods, leave the lorry separately, deliberately walking apart in an attempt to avoid suspicion.

Despite the quality of the video, which at first viewing was thought to be too indistinct for an identification of the suspects, Commander Tucker believes the robbers are distinct enough to be identified.

The first suspect, who got out of the driver's side of the lorry, is about 5 foot 8 inches tall, and stockily built. He was wearing a slate grey anorak, with hood, and dark trousers.

The passenger was slimmer, and slightly taller, about 5 foot 9 inches, and was wearing light-blue jeans and a blue and white mottled jacket with a hooded jogging top.

If you were in the area, and saw the two men leave the lorry at different times, one walking about 30 metres in front of his accomplice, could you please contact the police on 337 4141. Your calls will be dealt with in the strictest confidence. According to the police, the lorry, stolen in the Midlands last month, had been repainted from white to blue, a very deep blue, and fitted with false registration plates.

A tip-off, the night before, that a robbery somewhere in the city was imminent, included descriptions of three suspects, but police were unable to say if the descriptions given the previous evening matched those of the two men in the lorry.

And finally, sport. The European Cup winners . . .

2 Museum visit   page 99

Good afternoon, ladies and gentlemen. It is with great pleasure that I welcome you to our city's new Museum of Industrial and Rural Life. The museum provides us with a unique historical record of industrial and agricultural life in the area – all in the heart of the city!

Here, you'll find a wonderful collection of industrial and agricultural bygones, some dating back 200 years, which reflect the history of our area over the last two centuries. Many of the exhibits have been restored to full working order.

Until recently, the area was dominated by agriculture, and the rural industries and traditions which are associated with it. The museum's significant collections bring this heritage back to life with a fascinating blend of working and static displays.

From early times, good communications with the rest of the country have led to industrial prosperity for the area. One example of such communications was the Roman road, Watling Street, which passed nearby.

Later, canals came to bring new prosperity, and then the railways.

Transport is a strong theme which will recur throughout your visit.

Good transport systems encouraged local industries, especially those related to agriculture and the museum has collections of national significance from many of these.

Local people, too, have changed history and the museum will introduce you to these and other local celebrities.

The displays, with all items collected locally, show what local life used to be like. Many displays of local items are 'in context' and show, for example, a blacksmith's forge, wheelwright's, printer's and cobbler's workshops. Working machinery brings these displays alive.

Whatever your interest, we hope the museum will have something for you.

So, let's go and make our first journey into the past . . .

3 Baltic cruise   page 99

Although it never has won (and probably never will win!) the title, Stockholm is a serious contender for 'The World's Most Beautiful Capital'. For it certainly is with its elegant seafront framing clear blue waters. Where Lake Malaren meets the Baltic Sea, numerous islands skirt the shores, creating wonderful panoramas. From Stockholm, you can cruise to the splendours of Tsar Peter the Great's 'Window to the West', founded in the early 18th century. Elegant and supremely beautiful, imperial St. Petersburg stands on 101 islands, linked by rivers, canals and bridges.

Regent Travel offer cruises from only £537 from the 5th of February to the 16th of December, departing one day a week, on Thursdays only. Included in the Regent Travel package are: return scheduled flights between British airports and Stockholm; two nights' twin bed and breakfast accommodation in central Stockholm, at the 5-star Hotel Stella, located right in the heart of the city; and four nights' twin full board accommodation, based upon two people sharing an inside cabin, aboard the Baltic Line M/S Northern Star. You can upgrade this to an outside cabin if you choose, for an additional payment.

You depart on a Thursday on a choice of flights to Stockholm, where you will be staying for one night at the Hotel Stella.

On Friday the M/S Northern Star will sail at 16.00 hours. Before docking at St Petersburg at 17.30 on Saturday, you'll have time to enjoy all the facilities the Northern Star has to offer. Saturday and Sunday nights will be spent moored in St Petersburg, where, on Sunday, you'll be able to sample the delights the city has to offer as you will be free to do your own sightseeing.

On Monday you depart from St Petersburg at 16.00 hours for your return journey. There's a farewell party on board with live music. On arrival at Stockholm next day at 13.00 hours, you will be transferred to the Hotel Stella until your departure on Wednesday.

Our lines are now open for additional information concerning bookings etc. Please quote reference number 9500B – that's B for Bertie – when phoning.

And now I'll pass you back to John, who's waiting to give you that phone number, but remember the reference number 9500B . . .

4 National Asthma Campaign Open Day   page 100

Good morning, ladies and gentlemen. I am delighted to welcome you to the NAC's annual Open Day. Each spring, this Open Day provides the opportunity for our research committee, trustees, supporters and staff to come together to share the successes of NAC research and to learn more about the work that is going on.

Our expected research spending for this financial year is a staggering £2.1 million, an increase of over £250,000, a quarter of a million pounds, on the previous financial year – and we continue to spend more money on helping asthma sufferers than any other non-commercial organization in this country, and that is including the government!

Nevertheless, be assured that however much money is available for research, we will continue to adhere to our rigorous standards when it comes to research awards and will support only research which passes the review process – any project not passing this stage of vetting will not be considered for a research award.

As we hear today of the work that has been carried out by some of the most dedicated scientists in the country, we can feel rightly proud – proud of the contribution we have made in the fight against asthma, with all its human, social and financial costs.

So let us welcome this morning's speakers.

Tapescripts • Task bank 6C

First, Lucy Wiggs, who is standing in for Dr Gregory Stones. She is going to present, on behalf of Dr Stones, an up-date of 'Abnormal sleep in children with nocturnal asthma and the effects on the learning and behaviour of these children'.

And secondly, Dr Michael Ashmore, who will be talking about the effects of ozone on that asthma-related complaint, hay fever. Dr Ashmore will be referring specifically to hay fever symptom severity in a rural population, and how living in the countryside can produce similar adverse effects to those suffered by people living in towns. So let us welcome first of all Lucy Wiggs . . .

Activities for Part 3

1 Hats page 100

I=Interviewer, **P**=Paul Offord

I Rather than grow too big for their boots they have had to avoid letting success go to their heads at Olney Headware, the only manufacturer of men's hats in Luton, a traditional hat-making town.
After 75 years making Panama hats and a handful of other styles, including uniform hats, the company made its first take-overs in the late 1980s. The past few years have been excellent for business – sales have risen 60% in five years! I talked to Managing Director, Paul Offord.

P When the Panama boom started in the late 1980s, a number of other manufacturers took up the challenge. Many found they weren't up to the job, but a few have stayed. However, we're still the country's biggest manufacturer of genuine Panama hats. We use only hand-woven fibre imported from Ecuador, and in the meantime the two take-overs have meant we've increased our total range of headware to 500 different styles.

I What kind of styles prove the most popul . . .

P Well, we try to make our range a mix of classical and fashion items.

I Like the Panama.

P That's right . . . but, although the Panama has been made by Olney for many of the company's 80 years – and is now an established classic – it would be foolish to assume that it'll always remain as fashionable as it's been for the past five years.

I I believe 1989 was a significant year for the company, was it not?

P Absolutely. We changed the name from A. E. Offord, the family name, and poached the name Olney from a competitor – then we began a new policy of selling direct to the high street. We'd been selling to the trade for nearly 75 years, but for a variety of reasons, we decided to cut out wholesalers and go direct to the retailers.

I And was it a successful move?

P Initially, we thought it would be difficult opening up 500 accounts in shops all over the country. But, in fact, we received a very good reception in the retail sector. After 75 years in the trade we were pleased to find we were pretty well-known. A lot of our customers had been buying our hats under different names without realizing it! It was hard work legging it all over the country but well worth it!

I And what would you say was your greatest problem, if you have one?!

P One we're well used to dealing with: the necessity to carry a large stock. Hats are very light but bulky. We've had to acquire new buildings for warehousing. At the beginning of July we had nearly 4,000 hats, valued at approximately £150,000, in storage. Many have gone out now – but we need the space for the tweed hats and caps we're making for the autumn.

I Despite the prestige of its own-name hats in the high street, the company tries not to forget that the biggest single sector in its business is industrial headware, of which it makes 5,000 units a week.

P Many of our industrial headware products require far less skill than goes into making a Panama that retails at up to around £80. But in many ways they're the lifeblood of the company.

I Paul, thank you for talking to us and we wish you all the best in hat-making for the future.

P Thank you.

2 Saving Australia page 101

P=Presenter, **M**=Miranda Chitty, **C**=Cindy

P Miranda Chitty, winner of this year's *Young Travel Writer of the Year* competition, talks to one of the people she met in Australia.

M Cindy's hillside was no different from any other in New South Wales. Once covered with eucalyptus trees, it was originally cleared for farmland by white settlers. In 100 years, 30 million hectares of the state's forests have disappeared, half the total. Now, its harvests are dwindling. Once fertile land has now turned barren, and without trees Australian earth falls apart.
Cindy began planting at dawn. She's up to her knees in mud with rain streaming down her face. At this time of year New South Wales will get about 24 inches of rain in three months – more than London gets in a year. But it's a good time to plant saplings.

C After a while you don't wear clothes any more. For a start everything you wear is wet (my T-shirt's soaked already), and waterproofs only make you wetter – from sweat, that is.

M And today you're planting . . .

C . . . part of my 'Save Australia' crusade – I have to plant 100 trees today! It's a good time, you don't need to water them in and, anyway, too much sun stresses them out.

M You've been here for quite a while, years in fact, haven't you?

C Twelve – to be exact! I was born in Texas and I met Graham, he was a graduate in English, when we were both working on a commune in the United States.
We were two kids with a dream! We wanted to live off the land without damaging it, and only produce what rubbish we could deal with ourselves!

M And did it work out?

C Well, two years later we were riding across Australia on a battered motorbike looking for a piece of land! When we saw this piece of bare hillside – 18 acres it was – here in New South Wales, we knew that this was it!

M Did you have any problems buying it?

C The farmer was, was only too happy to sell! It was eroded . . . barren . . . not a living thing in sight, the valley was no use to anyone. There was no shelter – and it was the height of summer, with temperatures around 40 centigrade. We had to choose between buying a hammer, a crowbar, nails, timber or corrugated iron. We settled on the hammer and started looking for the rest.

M And where did you live?

C Under the stars! We demolished an old farmhouse in exchange for the salvage and began to build. I did most of the carrying and Graham wielded the hammer!

M And then?

C Well, we started planting with ten packets of seeds we'd bought in Melbourne. We didn't know that the top of the hill stays warm while the valley freezes. We just planted everything everywhere! I wanted to create what I call a permaculture – you know, where plants, animals and people live together in a sort of huddle – we do better like that!

M Uh huh

C And . . . believe it or not, the trees grew, the native animals started to come back and here we are now – a ranch. We have a ranch in a nice wooded valley, it's home to a dozen people and 20,000 trees!

3 Two-star chef page 102

A=Andrea, **M**=Marco

A When I made my first visit to two-star chef Marco at Chez Marco in Knightsbridge, I was fully aware of his reputation. He is, by all accounts, rude, brash and arrogant, famous for humiliating staff and throwing out diners. But he is also handsome, enthusiastic and the best young chef in the country, whose French cooking won him a Michelin Guide star at 25, and two stars at 27.
Marco, do you still live up to your reputation?

M My reputation is eight years old. A man changes in eight years!

A Would you say you've changed much physically in that time?

M Well, my long hair's gone, I've got rid of my spotty complexion but, as you can see from the bulge under my chef's tunic, I've put on weight!

A But you've expanded financially, too, haven't you?

M Absolutely. I own Chez Pierre in Chelsea Harbour, and, of course, this place.

A Which must keep you extremely busy!

M Indeed! I work here six days a week. People want to see me. I make a conscious effort to walk through the restaurant two or three times every night.

A And how do the customers take that? Apparently some are actually afraid of you.

M No, no, I normally have a joke with them! The days when customers came looking for a fight are over. In fact, I've only ejected two

142

people from the restaurant since it opened last year!
A And how did that come about?
M One was a food critic. His reviews attacked me personally, so I waited for his guest to go to the bathroom and I went over to him and said: 'I know your feelings towards me and I know you know mine. Finish your lunch at your leisure. There's no charge today. Don't come back.' Is that kicking a man out? That's being graceful!
A And the other?
M . . . was a rival chef! He was asked to close his menu and leave. He was very insulting to me.
A Hmm, and what about your famous temper, bullying the staff? Are they things of the past?
M Shouting's only necessary when you wish to regain control, my friend. A bully is a person who takes advantage of someone who's weak. I don't employ weak people. Only weak people should work with weak people.
A You have a trace of a Yorkshire accent. Were you brought up in that area?
M Well, yes, in fact. My mother was Italian but I was brought up in Leeds.
A And do you still consider yourself an . . . an . . . angry young man?
M It's very easy for the press to condemn me but I live by a code.
A A code?
M I've never forgotten anything anyone's done for me and I've never forgotten anything anyone's done against me. I always remind them what they've done. I don't look for an apology. I just remind them, but I'll never run down their name.
A And do you consider you've been successful? You're very satisfied with your success, aren't you?
M What makes success? I think success is made by arrogance. Where does arrogance come from? Insecurity. So arrogance is positive and not negative! So what comes after success? Greatness! But what makes greatness? Humility makes greatness.
A And do you have humility?
M Do I have humility? That I cannot say!
A And what follows greatness?
M Retirement!
A Well, I have to report that my supper was a triumph: red mullet soup followed by lobster salad, followed by olive-encrusted lamb, followed by apricot soufflé and hand-made chocolates. And I have to admit, I do not exaggerate when I say that it was the best meal of my life!

4 Touring holiday page 103

I=Interviewer, J=Janey, G=Gary, O=Oliver

I Tempo Tours do it faster, or so they say! I talked to three tourists on the Tempo Tour – seven countries in 12 days! Oliver, do you think you've got to know Europe in 12 days?
O Well, seven countries, 2,700 miles – that's why it's called the Tempo Tour! I wouldn't say I've got to know it well, but I certainly know more than I did before I came!
I But isn't it ever so annoying when you can't get off the bus because you've absolutely *got* to see Rome in two hours?
O Well, that wasn't a problem. When your time is limited, you have to try and fit everything in, I suppose – and we're used to travelling long distances in Australia!
I But what if a particular place is really beautiful? Janey?
J Well, I would have liked to stay in some places longer. But it was the first time Gary and I had left the States and so this was the right trip for us to get an impression of Europe – just to whet our appetites!
I And where would you wish yourselves back to, if you had the chance to spend just another five minutes in Europe?
O Florence, to see Michelangelo's *David* again!
I Erm, how was the food? Gary?
G Swiss chocolate, fantastic! I always get an allergy from American chocolate. But in Switzerland I could eat white chocolate for the first time in my life. Nestle's *Galak*. That's one name I'll never forget.
J And you could eat cheese!
G That's right! I have this allergy to chemically treated food. In Los Angeles I can spend hours trying to find cheese or an apple that hasn't been pumped full of something or other. It's great just to be able to go into a shop without having to spend hours researching what's in the apple!
J And the herbs! Have you ever tasted a pizza with fresh herbs? The difference is like . . . day and night!
I Did you miss anything?
J Sure. Ice cubes. I just cannot understand how you can serve a cola in the summer without ice cubes. Two minutes in the sun and the stuff is cooking. At home we even put ice cubes into the wine.
I And what about McDonald's?
J We went once. But we have McDonald's in the US too. We came here to learn about European culture!
I And what do you think about Europeans now?
J Well, we kind of expected them to be cool and unfriendly – not interested in Americans, I guess! Interested in money, not people. But everybody we met was really nice and helpful . . . some of them were . . . well . . . they're pretty wonderful people! Even the hotel staff!
I But . . . Is 12 days really enough to see Europe?
J Well, we only had two weeks' vacation.
G Yeah, like nearly all Americans. That's why we're so hectic!
I And how are the people in Europe different from Americans?
G I think maybe Americans are more materialistic. Look at the store opening times – say you want to buy a cuckoo clock, but in Europe you never get what you want because the stores close for lunch. These people consider their break more important than just money, money, money.
I Er . . . how did you prepare for the trip?
O I didn't really. It was important to me to come without preconceptions.
G We bought some guide books to read on the plane. But we flew business class and you know what that's like – you get so much food and drink thrown at you – you just don't get to do anything else!
J We did pick up a couple more guide books here so we have great memories, just in case the pictures don't work out!
I Did you pick up any souvenirs?
O I picked up some clothes in Rome.
J I bought some crystal in Venice. A cuckoo clock, leather bags in Italy. Oh, and some souvenir coffee spoons. I collected so many in the States I just had to do the same in Europe.
I And what have Europeans got that you haven't?
J Well, in Munich, I was struck by the clothes for older ladies. At home it's almost impossible to find something made with my age group in mind. In Munich the shop windows were full. Stylish things but not boring. Unfortunately I wasn't able to pick anything up as we were there on a Sunday.
O I was most impressed by the classy cars. BMWs, or a Mercedes on every street corner. But – no Cadillacs. I guess that's because the streets are too narrow.
I Well, thanks for talking to me – and have a great trip back home!
O/J Thanks very much.

Activities for Part 4

1 Relationships page 104

1 and 6
We've known each other since we were at primary school together. We're very close. We've always done everything together; dressed in the same way, had the same hairstyle. I shouldn't be surprised if we end up going to the same university – we're very fond of each other, you see.

2 and 7
The thing I remember most about him was this dreadful habit of smoking a pipe. You'd arrive there in the morning and be greeted by this curtain of tobacco smoke pouring out of his room. It used to make me so angry. All his employees were non-smokers, you see – I used to start the day in a really bad temper and it would last all day long!

3 and 8
I looked upon her as one of my best friends – and now she's left, I feel very bitter. I know deep down she had to go, have her own life . . . but I only had her – my husband died shortly after she was born. I suppose the real problem is that I miss her. We didn't have well, the usual 'generation gap' arguments. She was always so good, and now I feel she's abandoned me!

4 and 9
What I always say is 'there are plenty more fish in the sea!'. You've got to look on the bright side, haven't you? That's the way she wanted it . . . Shame about all those presents, though. Had to give them all back. She kept the ring, mind you!

Never mind! I've put it all behind me. Look to the future – that's my motto!

5 and 10
I really didn't know her very well at all. We lived too far apart to form any lasting kind of relationship. And she was quite old when she had my mother. But she was a gentle soul. The kind of person who makes you long for days gone by when you think of her. You know, smells of bread baking in the oven – feelings of security, being safe.

2 Class distinction   page 105

1 and 6
Don't you agree that you're in control of your own life and you can do what you want? I didn't go to a private school. I was brought up in a fairly poor area, but I've been quite successful. I used to design gardens but now I run a specialist service in computers. I know people who've been sent to private schools and have ended up doing nothing with their life! If we could afford to send our children to a private school, we would, but it's more important that the family has a balanced existence.

2 and 7
I'd like to have been an artist, you know, bettered myself! And I still sketch now, if I've got an hour to spare – but I haven't got time to do any proper painting and drawing. Well, I left school straight away. I was a bit of a fool because I could have gone on. Now I can't afford to re-educate myself – I earn about £7 an hour – in fact you get paid by the minute on the production line. If you're five minutes late, you miss five minutes pay!

3 and 8
I was brought up in the south west but I've lived here in Liverpool for six years. I couldn't go back, it's too far for the kid's father, my ex-husband, to see them at weekends. Anyway, my mum and dad couldn't help – they haven't got two pennies to rub together.
I never go out – don't like to on my own, and anyway, I can't afford to. I'd love a TV but we haven't got one. Suppose I feel bitter in some ways, really.

4 and 9
I deal with a broad cross-section of people and after 15 years or so working, the view you form of people is far more meritocratic than based on class: for example, are they people you respect, trust, find interesting? I lend money to medium-sized companies and people running those aren't upper-middle class. But sometimes I'm embarrassed by the way I speak. In a room full of industrialists, for example, it can be a disadvantage. It's often taken by some as projecting a form of arrogance.

5 and 10
I suppose we're thought of as snobbish, and there is a lot of truth in that. But it's a strong element of human character and other countries have just as much snobbery. Still, the problems in this country are not really to do with class. I do think one of the basic things that is wrong now is the breakdown of the family. Perhaps people think the grass is greener elsewhere – money and privilege bring happiness! And we, well, we, we haven't exactly set a happy example in all this! It's not that easy having a title in this day and age!

3 Food   page 106

1 and 6
Some girls arrive when we open, do three hours training on the trot and then work their muscles individually with weights. They drink water but you never see then eat anything. They're hyperactive, don't eat or sleep properly and eventually end up in hospital. They think they're normal and you're abnormal!

2 and 7
Some people swear by their recipes more frequently than they do by any volume of religious testament or law. And all cooks have their favourite works of reference. *Modern Cuisine* may not find itself on everybody's kitchen shelf but that is not to deny its influence. The dishes are more balanced, the flavours are more distinctive and the textures lighter – this is enough to make *Modern Cuisine* the greatest collection of recipes of the century!

3 and 8
The cows' milk may not be safe to drink but, for the elderly population, the comforts of home outweigh the risks involved. Slowly the evacuees, all elderly and most of them women, are beginning to return to the area. Most supplement weekly deliveries of food with produce and livestock raised on the polluted land.

4 and 9
We humans soon found we were at our most efficient when we operated as a hunting pack. In this way we were able to turn our attention to bigger prey - but the meat was too tough for our small jaws. We entered the époque of the human chef – sliced and cooked meat became easy to consume. We adapted the food to our teeth.

5 and 10
We were eager to investigate and photograph the feeding patterns of the box jellyfish but we faced serious problems. The animals appear and disappear unpredictably in the water. Studying them in nature would be impractical – and, to add to our dilemma, most won't eat in captivity.

4 Coping with the unexpected   page 107

1 and 6
Well, I was in the toilet actually when everything started shaking. Apparently we'd hit some turbulence. Anyway, as I made my way back down the aisle, I fell and twisted my ankle. I would have been all right if I'd been in my seat. I'm used to this kind of thing as I do a lot of travelling so it doesn't bother me at all – but it was being on my feet just at that very moment, that's what did it!

2 and 7
We were travelling up to the fifth floor – I don't like escalators, they're too slow, so I always look for an alternative if possible. Anyway, we'd almost arrived at the 4th floor when the thing just stopped dead. Luckily there were four of us and somebody said, 'Don't worry! There's always an emergency button in these contraptions.' Luckily for us, he was right and ten minutes later we emerged safe and sound!

3 and 8
They were showing this scene of someone skiing. We all had to put on special glasses and then, suddenly, the skiers seemed to, well, sort of invade the room! The special effects were fantastic, you really felt as if you were there with them, particularly with this new 'all-round' sound they have nowadays. Anyway it was so realistic I vowed I would never take up the sport, if that's what it's really like!

4 and 9
There was this kind of indoor fountain, right next to our table – really beautiful, it was! And everything was perfect, a real celebration! Goodness knows what it must have cost – the service was absolutely superb, background music perfect – and then suddenly I knocked over a bottle. I was so embarrassed I didn't know where to put myself. I'm not joking! I nearly ran out of the place – but they might have thought I was trying to escape without paying the bill!

5 and 10
We were having sandwiches and cakes – a simple sort of meal we'd taken with us – but it was a beautiful day, you know, sun shining, bees buzzing, the odd fisherman further downstream looking at us in a rather disapproving way – we were making too much noise! Suddenly the heavens opened and down it came. The locals must have had a field-day watching us hurrying for shelter!

ANSWER KEY

1 SPEAKING

1A Getting to know you

1.0 page 6

Finding out if people know each other
Have you two been introduced? and *We haven't been introduced* sound too formal for this particular situation.
Had you met each other ... sounds rather 'heavy' for this kind of interaction.

2.0 page 7

A formal: level 5
use of *Mr* and *Miss*, *I would like to introduce you to* and the expression *How do you do?*
context: possibly two examiners and two candidates.

B less formal: level 3 / 4
use of first names and family names, *Good morning* and *Hello*
context: possibly two examiners and two candidates.

C informal; level 1 / 2
use of first names only and *Hi! (there!)*
context: possibly four students.

2.1 page 7

Suggested tone of expressions:
1 formal 2 formal 3 less formal
4 less formal but with first names only
5 informal 6 informal

2.2 page 7

Introducing other people and responding appropriately
Suggested combinations:
A *I'm Maria and this is Louis.*
B *Hi there! Good to see you!*
A *Good morning / afternoon / evening. I'm Dr, Mr, Mrs, Miss ___ and I would like to introduce you to my colleague Mr, Mrs, Miss ___*
B *How do you do?*
A *How do you do?* or *Pleased to meet you. Delighted to make your acquaintance* is rather formal.
A *I'm Maria Monteno and this is my colleague Louis Ferrand.*
B *Hello.*
Ms is rarely used in spoken English but it is often preferred as an alternative to *Mrs* or *Miss*, which denote married or single status.
Delighted to make your acquaintance sounds rather formal and somewhat 'flowery' for general introductions and responses.
a formal b informal c less formal
d less formal e less formal

3.0 page 8

Check the tapescript (on page 129) to see how much of the information you managed to note down correctly. 'Cold listening' like this can be difficult because there is no set task, no indication of what to listen for. Also, the memory load is high, it is difficult to remember all the detail and there is not enough time to write it all down.

3.1 page 8

Finding out about people
How much money do you earn? might be considered an invasion of privacy.

4.0 page 9

A The vowel sounds are:
1 /æ/ /e/ /ɪ/ /ɒ/ /ʌ/
2 /eɪ/ /iː/ /aɪ/ /əʊ/ /juː/
3 /æ/ /e/ /ɪ/ /ɒ/ /ʌ/
The second vowel in all five words is /ə/.
4 /eɪ/ /iː/ /aɪ/ /əʊ/ /juː/
The second vowel in all five words is /ə/.
A silent *e* on the end of a word of one syllable ending in one consonant makes the vowel before it 'say its alphabet name' i.e. A, I, O, U. e.g. *hate, time, hope, huge*
In one-syllable words where the last consonant is doubled before adding an ending beginning with a vowel, there is a short vowel sound, e.g. *wrapped, letter, fitted, rotten, running*.
In one-syllable words where the last consonant is not doubled when adding an ending beginning with a vowel, there is a long vowel sound, e.g. *making, writing, joking, tubing*.

B The words in column 1 all have the vowel sound /ɪ/.
Those in column two have /iː/.

4.1 page 9

1 Hart 2 Welt 3 Manton 4 Gracelands
5 Roland 6 Pond

1B People and places

1.0 page 10

Speculating
One can't rule out the possibility that ... sounds too formal.
Who knows? sounds abrupt and too informal.
might expresses probability / possibility.
could expresses probability / capability.
must expresses a logical explanation.

Pictures of the same person are:
A, G and I   B, C and F   D, E and H

1.1 page 11

1h bushy eyebrows 2g/e straight hair / nose
3g curly hair 4c/f oval / round face / eyes
5b rosy cheeks 6d slim build
7e turned-up nose 8a handlebar moustache
9j well built 10i of medium height

2.1 page 13

Describing location
The examiner would not be interested in knowing that something in the picture was *two centimetres from the left- / right-hand side* as it is not this kind of precise description that examiners are looking for. If you are comparing two pictures and need to explain where people or objects are, it is important to do this correctly, of course. If you make mistakes, this may create a negative impression of your ability in the examiner's mind. However, examiners usually ask for an interpretation of a picture and a more global description of photographs used in Part 2.

Describing similarities and differences
compared could be followed by *with*

2.2 page 14

Location of bank: Kingston High Street
Time of robbery: 2.30
Number of suspects: 3
Other customers saw a woman giving something to two men in the queue
Amount stolen: £15,000
Alarm raised by bank staff
Gang escaped in car driven by a woman

2.3 page 14

1 an ármed róbbery 2 a secúrity fírm
3 the Hígh Stréet bánk 4 machíne gúns
5 their áfternoon delívery 6 the secúrity gúards 7 the bánk clérks 8 the alárm bútton
9 a gétaway cár 10 dóuble yéllow línes
11 a tráffic wárden 12 a párking tícket

1C/D Jobs and training

1.0 page 16

Giving your opinion
Personally, I haven't the faintest idea about ... sounds rather rude and off-hand and suggests you have nothing else to say.
I'm quite convinced that ... expresses a very strong opinion.

145

Key • Module 2A

Asking for the opinion of others

Any comments? is often used when addressing a group of people in a more formal situation e.g. a meeting.

Would you care to comment on . . .?
What are your views on . . .? are often used when addressing an individual in a more formal situation e.g,. a TV interview with a politician.

What / How about you?
Would you agree with that?
What's your opinion?
What do you think . . .? are more suitable for an informal exchange of ideas.

1.1 page 17

Expressing preferences

There's no comparison between . . . and . . . sounds like a simple contrast but expresses a very strong preference.

Give me . . . any time! is more colloquial and would be used in an informal conversation.

2.1 page 18

1 mathematics   2 Chicago   3 7 Grade 'A'
4 maths and computing   5 maths   6 America
7 are good at   8 making big decisions

Money prompted Simon's decision to move in 1986 : the interviewer said he was part of the 'brain drain' – the emigration of intelligent people to another country to earn more money or get a better job – and Simon himself said 'the money offered to me in America proved impossible to resist.'
He keeps in touch with his friends by using e-mail (electronic mail) and listening to the BBC.

2.2 page 18

If you are unsure about the pronunciation, word stress or meaning for any of these words, consult the *Oxford Advanced Learner's Dictionary*.

2.3 page 19

1 rewards   2 grain   3 hedge   4 recoiling
5 poor   6 vague   7 believe   8 dejected
9 resist   10 nail

3.0 page 19

Disagreeing politely

You must be joking! and *You can't be serious!* sound rather insulting and dismiss the other person's point of view.
All the other expressions are more diplomatic.

The methods in the pictures for comparison are: studying alone, or with a private teacher; training with a computer, or practical experience in the workplace; training with a small or large group of people.

3.1 page 20

Admitting that you might be mistaken

All right – you win! sounds rather defeatist and would be used at the end of an argument.
Fair enough! is colloquial and concedes that the other person has a point.
I hadn't thought of . . . in that way.
Come to think of it you might be right.
I must admit it's true that . . .
I suppose you're right. are all used to suggest that you might possibly have made a mistake.
You're quite right, of course. admits quite freely that you were wrong.

3.2 page 20

Commenting on something you know nothing about

I have a sneaking suspicion that . . . could suggest that you are about to criticize someone or something.
Search me!
Haven't a clue! sound off-hand and fail to develop the interaction. This prevents either student from continuing the conversation and thus showing what they can do in English. It could also offend the other person!
You must take up every opportunity in an interview situation to show the examiner what you can do. If the examiner has asked you a question, some response will be expected. A 'shut-down' strategy not only makes life difficult for the examiner, it jeopardises your chances of success!

Finding out if everyone agrees

Well, that's that then! sounds rather dismissive and very informal.
It would appear that we are in complete agreement. sounds rather too formal for this kind of discussion.
So we're agreed on . . .
It looks as if we all agree that . . .
Can I take it that everyone agrees that . . .?
Are we all in agreement?
We appear to agree on . . . could be used diplomatically to draw a discussion to a close.

2 LISTENING

2A Sorry, I didn't quite catch that!

1.0 page 23

Speculating about what you hear

sounds + adjective, e.g. *sounds strange*
sounds like + noun, e.g. *sounds like a plane*
sounds as if + sentence, e.g. *sounds as if someone is talking*

These are the sounds. You can make your own suggestions about where you might hear them.
1 engaged telephone signal   2 pneumatic drill
3 lawn mower cutting grass   4 car brakes screeching   5 helicopter   6 background chatter at a party   7 fans screaming at a rock concert   8 washing machine spinning
9 glass smashing   10 a dog barking

1.1 page 24

Suggested answers are given for each extract in the order: speaker, sound, place, situation.
1 reporter
  aircraft taking off or landing
  airport
  possibly a strike or disruption of services
2 motorist
  traffic
  possibly a motorway
  car broken down
3 car owner
  car alarm
  possibly a car park
  car owner apprehending a thief who is breaking into his car
4 employee at a large store
  crackle and tone of a public address system
  supermarket or department store
  another employee is being called, possibly to help exchange goods
5 sports correspondent
  football crowd
  large football ground
  important football match
6 dog owner
  children playing
  park
  owner throwing a stick for the dog to run after, near a children's playground

2.0 page 24

1 c   2 b   3 e   4 a   5 f

2.1 page 24

1 A protest about people being threatened with eviction from their homes because of a proposed new road.
2 An advert for a trip in a hot air balloon.
3 An advert for a new vacuum cleaner which can do many different jobs.
4 A financial report about a company about to go bankrupt.
5 An announcement saying that a short holiday in Holland will include an excursion to see the bulb [tulip] fields where the flowers are grown.
Possible key words are marked on the tapescript on page 130.

3.0 page 25

Finding out about correct spelling

a ~~acommodation~~ accommodation
b conscience ✓ c benefited ✓ or benefitted
d professional ✓ e gauge ✓
f ~~embarassment~~ embarrassment
g comparable ✓ h ~~decieve~~ deceive
i courteous ✓ j guarantee ✓
k ~~wether~~ whether, weather
l ~~busness~~ business   m feasible ✓
n accustomed ✓

These are the possible spellings of the words on the tape. Use a dictionary to check the meanings.
1 ceiling / sealing   2 seize / seas / sees
3 tear / tier   4 roll / role   5 story / storey
6 flaw / floor   7 know / no   8 threw / through
9 weight / wait   10 bear / bare   11 choose / chews   12 pear / pair / pare

Module 2B • Key

3.1 page 26

1 /ræt/ /reɪt/ Silent E on the end of a word makes the vowel in front sound as it does in the alphabet, i.e. /eɪ/ /iː/ /aɪ/ /əʊ/ /juː/
2 /raɪt/ /ˈrɪtən/ In one-syllable words with a short vowel sound, double the last consonant before adding an ending beginning with a vowel.
3 /kənˈsiːt/ /brˈliːv/ I before E when the sound is 'ee' except after C. *Seize* is an exception to this rule!
4 /ɒɪuː/ /ɪʌf/ /ˈθʌɪə/ There is no rule for this one!
5 /ˈnɒlɪdʒəbl/ /rɪˈsiːvəbl/ /ˈnəʊtɪsəbl/ Keep the final E when adding endings to keep the /s/ or /dʒ/ sounds on words ending in CE and GE (Unless the ending begins with E, I or Y).
6 /elf/ /elvz/ /brˈliːf/ /brˈliːfs/ When a word ends in F, change the F to VE before adding S, *belief* is an exception!
7 /pəˈteɪtəʊ/ /pəˈteɪtəʊz/ /piːˈænəʊ/ /piːˈænəʊz/ Some nouns ending in O add ES in the plural but some just add S. Commonly used words assimilated into English add ES e.g. *potatoes*, less common words add S e.g. *pianos*.
8 /fraɪ/ /ˈfraɪɪŋ/ If a word ends in a consonant plus Y, change the Y to I before adding any ending unless the ending begins with I.
9 /ɪkˈsiːd/ /ɪɡˈzɪst/ The sound /s/ is written C after X but the sound /z/ requires no C.
10 /ˈkwɒrəl/ /ˈkwɒrəld/ The letter Q must always be followed by U plus a vowel. In words of more than one syllable, if the last syllable ends in one vowel plus L, e.g. EL, AL, then the L is doubled before adding an ending beginning with a vowel, e.g. *rivalled*, *travelling*.
11 /əˈkædəmɪ/ /ˌɒkəməˈdeɪʃn/ Most words beginning with the sounds /æk/ or /ək/ are spelt ACC, but *academy* is an exception.
12 /maɪ/ /ˈmaɪlɪdʒ/ Keep the final E when adding endings to make the meaning clear and avoid mispronunciation, e.g. *dye – dyeing*, *hoe – hoeing*.

4.0 page 26

1 Roland Bloom
2 96 1980
3 fifties
4 owed back-taxes
5 property
6 its closure
7 gas light
8 the ground floor   three-storey   town house
9 intact
10 very cross   it's unfair

Exam practice   page 28

1 farmer
2 (AD) 383
3 (supermarket) plastic bags
4 his (own) land
5 informed the authorities
6 prosecution
7 farm tools
8 dig up
9 declare their discoveries
10 more than / over 300,000 / three hundred thousand objects
11 thanked
12 the law

2B Leisure activities and holidays

1.0   page 29

1 hiking   2 pony-trekking   3 diving
4 hot air ballooning   5 white-water canoeing (on fast moving turbulent rivers)   6 pot-holing
7 bungee jumping (jumping from a high place, usually a bridge or a crane, attached to an elastic rope)   8 aerobics

1.1   page 29

pot-holing, bungee jumping and aerobics are mentioned.

1.2 and 1.3   pages 29 and 30

A Activity
B Place
C Cost
D For further information

1 Archery
2 after 4 p.m.
3 Swindon
4 office hours
5 Synchronised swimming
6 annual subscription
7 stamped addressed envelope
8 £16 a day
9 Ballroom dancing
10 Middlesex

1.4   page 30

Suggested answers
a   young people on school holidays
b   catchy and amusing alliteration and rhyming, e.g. *boring in Goring*, *cheesed off in Cheshire*, and informal, chatty, 'teenage' style language, e.g. *ace sports*
c   young trendies – young people who like to follow trends in what is fashionable, e.g. in activities and clothes
d   enthusiastic 'sporty' types

2.0   page 30

1 a páckage hóliday
2 a tíme-share próperty
3 an ísland crúise
4 a bárgain bréak
5 a théme park
6 a cúltural tour
7 a cámp site
8 a tóurist tráp
9 a flý-dríve hóliday
10 a róund trip

2.1   page 31

a 2 ticks   b 5 ticks   c 4 ticks   d 2 ticks
e 6 ticks   f 2 ticks
All the information is referred to several times but the important information which it wants the listener to remember and be attracted by is repeated most often – this is part of the selling technique.

3.0   page 31

a   having a ball
b   travelling around under your own steam
c   leaving all your troubles behind you

3.1   page 31

1 B   2 A   3 C   4 C

3.2   page 32

> **Advising someone (not) to do something**
> *On no account should you…* sounds too impersonal and too formal.
> *'You'd be crazy not to…'* sounds very familiar and somewhat offensive.
> *'Why on earth don't you…?'* sounds colloquial and suggests that the speaker is irritated.
> *'It's high time you (did)…'* implies that the listener has not been doing the right thing.
> You could complete the sentence *I'd recommend* with, for example, *the cafe opposite the cinema* or *that you (should) go to that one*.

> **Putting forward another point of view**
> *Surely you can't really believe…?* and *Look, nobody in their right mind would think that…* sound insulting.

Exam practice   page 33

1 deck chair   2 other nations   3 drive (very) slowly   4 on mountain roads   5 the food
6 complain   7 Scotland   8 friendly
9 a camera   10 one nation / one country / the same

2C Mind over matter

1.0   page 34

1 mn
2 colours of the rainbow
3 Great Lakes of North America
4 US states which border Mexico
5 US states bordering Canada
6 Colombia
7 Ecuador
8 a coastline
9 rhythm

1.1   page 34

1 *Richard Of York Gained Battles In Vain* for red, orange, yellow, green, blue, indigo and violet
2 *Super Man Helps Every One* for lakes Superior, Michigan, Huron, Erie and Ontario
3 California, Arizona, New Mexico and Texas
4 *Well, I Must Not Mislead* for Washington, Idaho, Montana, North Dakota, and Minnesota
5 *British Petroleum* for Bolivia and Paraguay

1.2   page 34

Possible answers
a   MAT (west to east)
b   SUE or (south to north) USE

147

Key • Module 2D

2.0 page 35

A Suggested answers
5 **The British are happier using** a person's **first name.**
6 **Americans like** being asked **personal questions.**
7 You should **analyse your own style** of speaking carefully.

B
1 No 2 Yes 3 Yes 4 No 5 No 6 Yes
7 Yes

2.1 page 35

> **Correcting what is not accurate**
> *That's absolute rubbish!* sounds abrupt and rude.
> *Forgive me if I contradict you but . . .* sounds too formal.

Corrected statements
1 It highlights the differences between male and female styles of conversation.
4 Men seem distant because they fail to realise the need for 'human interest' questions.
5 The British feel uncomfortable using a person's first name straightaway.

3.0 page 35

A Suggested words to highlight
3 When a mother asked her adult son, who had a full-time job, to contribute to the household expenses, what did he do?
  A He **moved** into a place of his own.
  B He reluctantly **agreed** to **pay** rent.
  C He **pretended** he had **not heard** her.
  D He **left** the **matter** open.
4 What is the difference between girls' and boys' conversational styles?
  A **Boys** give **girls** direct **commands.**
  B **Girls** get their own way by **making suggestions.**
  C **Boys** give **each other options** when deciding what to do.
  D **Girls** are **more likely** to be **assertive** than boys.

B
1 B 2 C 3 D 4 B

3.1 page 36

In the first exchange the employee agrees to think about helping, not to help, but the employer assumes that he has agreed to help. In the second exchange the mother assumes her son has agreed to pay as he will only be there for a short time, while the son has merely acknowledged the fact that she has asked him and feels he has not agreed to anything.

3.2 page 36

A Suggested information to highlight
1 How should the cake shop owner give orders to the male employee?
  A **Insist** that he helps with the invoicing.
  B **Politely tell** him exactly what she wants him to do.
  C **Persuade** him over a period of time to do what she wants.
  D **Ask** him **directly why** he **won't do** what she asks.
2 How should the mother deal with her son?
  A **Insist** that he honours her wishes.
  B **Encourage** him to be more honest with her.
  C **Give** him a **deadline** to produce the money.
  D **Ask** him **directly when** she can expect a contribution.

B
1 B 2 D

Exam practice page 37

1 B 2 C 3 D 4 C 5 A

2D Today's technology

1.2 page 39

1 feel about paying 2 ripped off 3 by the retailers. 4 more or less fair. 5 are cheap.
6 put you off 7 Not at all! 8 Not really!
9 keen 10 gets boring 11 four to / and six weeks. 12 than two weeks.
Answers 1, 2, 3, 4, 6, 9, 10 and 11 needed changing or putting into a different context.

2.0 page 39

1 disapprove 2 disapprove 3 approve
4 approve 5 neutral 6 disapprove
7 approve 8 disapprove 9 approve

2.1 page 39

Suggested answers
1 parent 2 doctor 3 teenager 4 teenager
5 video manufacturer 6 parent 7 video manufacturer 8 doctor 9 teenager
(The policeman is not used)
Words which help identify the speakers
1 *my children* 2 *younger patients / suffering from 'photosensitive epilepsy'.* 3 *can't stop playing* 4 *like inviting friends* 5 *order replacements* 6 *young people / I / our house.*
7 *We / our games / help children* 8 *medical research we've been carrying out* 9 *I / bought / exciting*

2.2 page 40

1 console 2 strictly 3 violent 4 conducted
5 fighting 6 borrow

2.3 page 40

1–4 e f k h in any order
5–6 c i in any order
7 j
8–10 b d g in any order
(a is not used)

3.0 and 3.1 pages 41 and 42

See tapescript on page 134.

3.2 page 42

HOW TO SCORE
1 Score one for each
2 (a) 0 (b) 2 (c) 3
3 (a) 1 (b) 3 (c) 0
4 (a) 3 (b) 1 (c) 0
5 (a) 0 (b) 3 (c) 2
6 (a) 2 (b) 0 (c) 3
7 (a) 0 (b) 1 (c) 3
8 Score one for each

WHAT YOUR SCORE MEANS
0–5 Your antipathy to television is somewhat extreme!
6–10 Do you understand what your family and / or friends are talking about all the time?
11–15 You are a reasonably well-adjusted member of our TV-obsessed society.
16–21 Unless all your friends are as TV crazy as yourself you should begin to worry seriously about your social life. And how's your eyesight?
22–25 You are a TV fanatic, a hi-tech couch potato. Don't you have any friends?

Exam practice page 42

1 H 2 C 3 E 4 A 5 D 6 E 7 A 8 G 9 B
10 C

3 SPEAKING

What if . . .?

1.0 page 43

> **Talking about certainty, possibility and improbability.**
>
> *I doubt whether . . .*   improbable
> *I'm bound to . . .*   almost certain
> *There's a fairly good chance
>   of . . .*   possible
> *There's no doubt in my mind
>   whatsoever that . . .*   almost certain
> *I shouldn't be surprised if . . .*   possible
> *I'm absolutely convinced
>   that . . .*   almost certain
> *There's very little chance of . . .*   improbable
>
> Suggested completions
> *I doubt whether* + sentence, e.g. *I'll become*
> *I'm bound to* + infinitive, e.g *become*
> *There's a fairly good chance of* + gerund, e.g. *me / my becoming*
> *There's no doubt in my mind whatsoever that* + sentence, e.g. *I'll become*
> *I shouldn't be surprised if* + sentence, e.g. *I become / became*
> *I'm absolutely convinced that* + sentence, e.g. *I'll become*
> *There's very little chance of* + gerund, e.g. *me / my becoming*

2.0 page 44

Interpreting past ideas
It is reasonable to assume they thought life would / might . . . sounds formal and rather impersonal.
Dates the pictures were published:
Teacher 1940   Street 1895   City 1995

3.0 page 45

1 Y 2 N 3 N 4 Y 5 Y 6 Y

3.1 page 45

1 fínal   finálity
2 histórical   hístory
3 apocalýptic   apócalypse
4 capabílity   cápable
5 áctually   actuálity
6 cálculated   calculátion
7 retaliátion   retáliate

Module 3B • **Key**

3.2 page 45

1. What would have happened if the 1962 Cuban missile crisis had teetered over the edge?
2. What would have happened if the US had carried out its threat to bomb the Soviet missile sites?
3. What would have happened if subsequent retaliation had taken place?
4. What would have happened if mankind hadn't invented the wheel?
5. What would have happened if dinosaurs hadn't been wiped out?
6. What would have happened if the whole human race had remained vegetarian?
7. What would have happened if penicillin hadn't been discovered?
8. What would have happened if other animals had developed the same intelligence as human beings?

4.1 page 46

1 cash lump sum   2 travel alarm clock
3 telephone answering machine   4 save £25 a month   5 future profits   6 inflation

5.0 page 47

> **Expressing wishes and regrets**
> *If only . . . I wish . . . How I wish . . .* can be followed by the Past Perfect, the Past Simple, the Past Continuous, *could* but not *would*, e.g.
> *I had(n't) (done)*
> *I did(n't) (do)*
> *I was / were(n't) (doing)*
> *I could (do)*
> *Had I . . .* is part of a past conditional: *If I had* or *Had I realized, I would never have bought the car.* (Past Perfect + Past Conditional)
> *If only . . .* and *How I wish . . .* seem to be the most expressive.

3B Yesterday and today

1.0 page 48

Similarities: the church and the town hall.
Differences: the landscape, traffic signs, zebra crossing, car, war memorial.

1.1 page 49

> **Ways of linking contrasting ideas**
> *although / nevertheless* would be less appropriate for describing the differences between the two pictures, although they could both be used to add information to what has already been said, e.g. 'There is a church in both pictures, although it's difficult to see whether the church has changed or not.'

1.2 page 49

> **Giving yourself time to think**
> *. . . there can't have been . . .*
> *. . . there must have been . . .* offer a logical explanation.
> *. . . there might have been . . .*
> *. . . there could have been . . .* offer a possible explanation.
> *. . . there might have been . . .*
> It is just possible that this happened.
> *. . . there can't have been . . .*
> Surely this didn't happen
> *. . . there must have been . . .*
> Surely this happened
> *. . . there could have been . . .*
> It is just possible that this happened.

2.0 page 50

The Brighton Beach picture was drawn in 1907.

2.1 page 51

Suggested answers
1. Brighton invented the seaside.
2. A doctor wrote about the advantages of sea water for the health.
3. Enter the cold water and drink a pint of it.
4. To cure illnesses.
5. Because the water might be polluted.
6. Queen Victoria sold the Royal Pavilion.
7. She hated Brighton and the crowds of people near where she lived.
8. As a great palace of fun.

2.2 page 51

1 invénted	ínventory
2 expláined	explanátion
3 históric	hístory
4 publicátion	públish
5 advántages	advantágeous
6 várious	varíety
7 moderátion	móderate
8 mágnet	magnétic

3.0 page 52

> **Politely asking someone to repeat something**
> *Sorry, I couldn't hear what you said*, when something prevents you from hearing.
> *I'm so sorry, but I'm not sure I understood correctly . . .* sounds very polite indeed.
> *I'm sorry, I didn't quite catch that . . .*
> *Sorry – what was that again?*
> *Sorry – could you say that again, please?*
> *Sorry – I couldn't hear what you said.*
> *Could you repeat that, please?*
> are more informal.
> *I hate to interrupt but what did you say?*
> could sound rather rude if *what* was stressed too loudly.

3.1 page 54

> **Asking if someone agrees**
> *You agree, don't you?* expects the answer *yes*.
> *Wouldn't you say that . . .?* sounds as if you are trying to persuade someone to agree with you.
> *Surely you don't think that . . .?* implies that you do not believe what you are hearing.

3.2 page 54

1C   2E   3A   4D   5G

4.1 page 55

> **Comparing**
> *On the whole . . . By and large . . .* mean 'generally speaking'.
> *Come off it! There's no comparison between . . .* sounds rather rude and dismissive.

4.2 page 56

> **Explaining how you feel about something**
> *To be honest / The fact is . . .* are often used before a personal 'confession'.

3C/D Art and culture

1.0 page 58

> **Summing up**
> *Basically, it's a question of whether . . .* implies two possibilities.
> *So, to sum up . . .* might be used after rather a lengthy discussion.

The picture is advertising modern music.
'Lifeforms – 90 minutes of organic soundscapes redefining electronic modern classical ambient'
It is available on CD and cassette.

1.1 page 58

> **Saying you are interested**
> *I'm a bit of a fanatic* suggests you are crazy about something

> **Saying you are not interested**
> *. . . isn't my kind of thing at all* sounds very informal.
> *I couldn't care less about . . .* is rather abrupt and rude.

2.0 page 59

> **Saying something is (in)appropriate**
> *I wouldn't be seen dead in . . .* sounds very informal and rather dismissive.

2.1 page 60

> **Saying something is or isn't fashionable**
> *. . . went out with the ark!* suggests something is very old-fashioned.
> *is / are all the rage at the moment! . . .* suggests that something is extremely popular.
> *. . . is / are all the rage at the moment!*
> *. . . went out with the ark!*
> *. . . is / are 'in' this summer*
> are very informal.

3.0 page 60

> **Making a choice**
> *Definitely this one* would not impress the examiner as it gives you very little opportunity to show off your speaking skills and the examiner very little to assess you on.

Key • Module 4A

3.1 page 62

Arguing for
I'd certainly give . . .my support suggests you are approving someone else's proposal to do something.
I can't see anything against . . . conveys less than enthusiastic support.

Arguing against
I'm dead against sounds very informal.
I really couldn't condone . . . sounds rather formal.

4.0 page 64

The genuine picture is on the right. The other picture has been electronically 'refined'. The background has been changed, his hat is black and he has lost a hand. Apologies to Van Gogh!

4.1 page 64

A 1R 2N 3C 4C 5N 6N 7C 8N 9C 10R 11N 12R

B Information which gave clues:
1 'a castle in rural France'
3 'the biggest art scandal . . . for at least 20 years'
4 'When I get permission, I'll put on an exhibition for the press.'
7 'Mr Van Der Bergen started selling paintings and certificates of authenticity to galleries and auction houses in major German cities like Bonn, Cologne . . .'
9 'the local people didn't see him very often. He was occasionally spotted riding through the countryside on his bicycle . . .'
10 'the maximum sentence for forging artworks is only five years in jail, and he won't serve more than three if he's well-behaved.'
12 'the worst punishment Mr Van Der Bergen could receive could be the governor's eventual refusal of an urgent request for brushes, canvas and an easel!'

4 LISTENING

4A Achievements

1.0 page 66

1 the electric iron 2 the electric light bulb
3 the sewing machine 4 the pocket watch

1.1 page 66

1 1828 2 1914 3 an apprentice
4 a chemist 5 making photographic plates
6 carbon printing 7 Frances (Fransis) White, White's sister 8 Hanna(h) (White) (her sister)
9 7 10 light and electricity 11 first electric light bulb 12 Swan Electric Lamp Company
13 Thomas Edison / Tomas Eddison (any acceptable spelling correct) 14 honours

1.2 page 67

Possible answers
1 In the chemist's where he worked – she was the chemist's sister.
2 His first wife had died and he felt lonely. He fell in love with someone who reminded him of his wife.
3 They had never seen an electric light bulb before.
4 He improved Edison's design for a carbon filament lamp.
5 Edison was the first person to create electric light and he had obtained the patent for a carbon filament lamp.
6 Honorary degrees and prizes.

2.0 page 67

1 Thumping Good Read
2 enjoy reading / find entertaining
3 turn the page
4 for pleasure
5 later this year
The title means an exceptionally enjoyable book to read. *Thumping* is used colloquially to mean *big* or *prominent*.

2.1 page 68

1 snowdrift 2 has crashed / has been wrecked
3 dead 4 money / over $4 million 5 keep the money 6 (betrayed and) murdered 7 work of art 8 be friends 9 Great War 10 upside down 11 vote 12 a nurse 13 heroism
14 break the (solemn) vow

3.1 page 68

1 Sam Gray (or Grey) 2 a top male model
3 a top writer 4 more than just a handsome face

3.2 page 69

1 N 2 I 3 N 4 S 5 I 6 N 7 S 8 I
9 I

3.3 page 69

Correct words
1 *heights* instead of *highs*
2 *sights* instead of *sighs*
3 *snapped* instead of *snipped*
4 *globe* instead of *grove*
5 *despite* instead of *in spite*
6 *tea-stained* instead of *tea-strained*
7 *world* instead of *word*
8 *mortals* instead of *morals*
9 *contacts* instead of *contracts*
10 *career* instead of *carrier*

4.0 page 69

Question:
Has the course of events ever been changed significantly as a result of a letter written to, or published by, a national newspaper?

4.1 page 70

1 D 2 F 3 H 4 A 5 B 6 G 7 E
8 C

Exam practice page 70

1 improbable phrases 2 lifelike situations
3 mock-up 4 table 5 foreign language speakers 6 talented 7 (the) language unit manager 8 shorthaul 9 longhaul
10 'Tasterday'

4B Survival

1.0 page 71

The picture shows a 'recycled' cyclist and stresses the importance of recycling materials and resources.

1.1 page 71

Speaker 1
1C 2E 3G
Speaker 2
4B 5D 6H
Speaker 3
7A 8F
Point *I* is not made by any speaker.

2.0 page 72

1 feel, sleep and look better
2 mental and physical
3 anxious patients
4 (complicated / difficult) postures

2.1 page 72

A
Aerobic exercise	1F	2C
Alexander Technique	3A	4E
Relaxation tapes	5D	6H
Yoga	7B	8G

I is not needed.

B
Aerobic exercise	1E	2C
Alexander Technique	3B	4I
Relaxation tapes	5D	6G
Yoga	7H	8F

A is not needed.

2.2 page 73

See tapescript on page 137. *Tranquillizers* can also be spelt *tranquillisers* or *tranquilizers* (US).

3.0 page 73

1 attack (it) / not run away
2 too little about
3 organizing expeditions
4 quality of life
5 commercial tour companies
6 Albion Mountains
7 a member (of *Earthwatch*) / members

3.1 page 73

1 pérsecuted	persecútion
2 húman	humánity
3 díréct(adj.)	diréct (verb)
4 órganized	organizátion
5 prójects (noun)	projécts (verb)
6 scientific	scíentist
7 famíliar	familiárity
8 commércial	cómmerce
9 cómpany	compánion
10 accommodátion	accómmodate
11 réal	reálity
12 informátion	infórm

4.0 page 74

1 Y 2 N 3 Y 4 Y 5 Y 6 N 7 N 8 Y

Module 4C • **Key**

4.2 page 74

Saying you'd rather not
You can count me out! and *It seems a strange sort of thing to do, if you ask me.* express the most reluctance to join.
Actually, I don't really think I could find the time. offers an excuse for not joining.

Saying you aren't sure
Well, I'm in two minds about it really.
I can't make up my mind. suggest that the speaker might never get round to making a decision.

Saying you'd like to
Never in my wildest dreams did I imagine I'd . . . sounds too enthusiastic.
I think I might be able to work up some enthusiasm for the idea. suggests that the speaker is slightly less keen on the idea.

Exam practice page 76

1 military 2 the public 3 more members
4 professional 5 charities 6 large crowds
7 (charity) events 8 future

4C A question of gender

1.1 page 76

1 emotions 2 mathematical 3 verbal
4 in three dimensions 5 locations

2.0 page 77

The answers are given on the cassette as part of exercise 2.1, which follows.

2.1 page 78

1 Numbers 1 and 3 are the same
  41% of women and 64% of men scored correctly.
2 Perfect score: 20
  Average score for women: 15
  Average score for men: 12
3 Average score for women: 4.1 synonyms per word
  Average score for men: 2.2 synonyms per word

2.2 page 78

Statements 2, 4 and 5.

4.0 page 79

1 M   2 N   3 S   4 N   5 M   6 N   7 N
8 S   9 N   10 S 11 N 12 M 13 M
14 S 15 N 16 S

5.0 page 80

See tapescript on page 138. *Sensitized* can also be spelt *sensitised*.

Exam practice page 80

1 M   2 N   3 M   4 N   5 D   6 D   7 N
8 M   9 N

4D Points of view

1.0 page 81

Speaker 1   Boredom
Speaker 2   Pleasure
Speaker 3   Disbelief

1.1 page 81

	Fairly certain	Less certain
Speaker 1		✓
Speaker 2	✓	
Speaker 3	✓	
Speaker 4		✓
Speaker 5		✓
Speaker 6	✓	

2.0 page 82

Suggested answers
Speaker 1
 1 anger
 2 he's anti-sports
Speaker 2
 3 documentary, biography of biologist (Rupert Sheldrake)
 4 very good programme
Speaker 3
 5 cookery programme (set in Italy)
 6 disappointed
Speaker 4
 7 comedy quiz
 8 it wasn't funny, nobody answered the questions, everybody tried too hard to be funny
Speaker 5
 9 not satisfied, or angry
10 never accurate, too complicated, can't rely on it

3.0 page 83

Speaker 1   1C   2B
Speaker 2   3B   4A
Speaker 3   5A   6A
Speaker 4   7B   8A
Speaker 5   9B   10A

3.1 page 84

1 night   knight   7 so   sew   sow
2 days   daze   8 made   maid
3 great   grate   9 rights   writes
4 role   roll   10 new   knew
5 for   four   11 died   dyed
6 hours   ours   12 seen   scene

4.0 page 84

1C   2I   3D   4B   5H

4.1 page 84

1D   2C   3E   4G   5B

4.2 page 85

1 aided ('ed' pronounced 'id' after 't' or 'd')
2 lightweight (one word – although candidates would not be penalized for putting a hyphen in a compound word of this kind)
3 limbs (silent 'b')
4 rechargeable ('e' needed after 'g')
5 snoring (only one 'r')
6 wrecking (silent 'w')
7 harmful (only one 'l' in full when a compound)
8 children's education ('n' apostrophe 's')
9 annoying ('y' does not change before 'ing')
10 running (double 'n')
11 irresponsible (double 'r' needed)
12 mayhem (you might be able to guess – means 'violent or damaging action' – from the old French – similar to 'maim')

Exam practice page 85

Task one
1G   2E   3C   4B   5A
Task two
6C   7F   8H   9G   10E

5 PAPER 5 TASK BANK

Activities for Part 2

4 Ball control   page 89

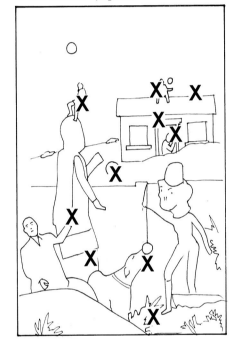

Activities for Parts 3 and 4

3 Can competition   page 92

5 Installation art   page 94

A Maid of the mist
B This inability to escape
C Lapwing, redwing, fieldfare (these are wild birds)
D Sight unseen

151

Key • Task bank 6A

6 PAPER 4 TASK BANK

Activities for Part 1

1 Brooklyn Center schools' programs page 96

1 (the) urban countryside
2 age
3 immigrated / emigrated (to America)
4 unique
5 subjects on the curriculum / curriculum subjects
6 training and development workshops
7 walking
8 theme
9 Environmental and science
10 Summer day camps

2 High-tech spy page 97

1 green cameras
2 two / 2 years
3 Denver University
4 one third / a third / 1/3 of a second
5 accident levels
6 48%
7 gross polluters
8 in California
9 regular offenders

3 Artist's eye page 97

1 poor colour vision 2 violent blue 3 his late paintings 4 the majority of us 5 brownish 6 more yellow 7 darker 8 slashed several canvases 9 in direct sunlight 10 foggy 11 died

4 Theme park page 98

1 (the) huge queues
2 the following day
3 resting / relaxing
4 in the Towers / park (itself)
5 indoor (children's) play area
6 Peter Rabbit Ice Show
7 the Haunted House
8 when you leave
9 raincoat
10 attendances
11 (a fair bit) cheaper

Activities for Part 2

1 City robbery page 98

1 week ago 2 200 metres 3 a lorry
4 robbery occurred 5 walk together
6 identify the robbers 7 slimmer and taller
8 (deep) blue 9 night before

2 Museum visit page 99

1 industrial and agricultural / rural life
2 200 years / two centuries
3 communications
4 transport
5 local people / celebrities
6 collected locally
7 working machinery

3 Baltic cruise page 99

1 most beautiful capital
2 St Petersburg
3 Regent Travel
4 in (the) city centre / in (the) heart of (the) city
5 Outside cabins
6 on Thursday(s)
7 St Petersburg
8 your own sightseeing
9 (a) farewell party
10 reference number 9500B

4 National Asthma Campaign Open Day page 100

1 year / spring
2 research
3 £250,000 / a quarter of a million pounds
4 research award
5 proud
6 Dr Gregory Stones
7 nocturnal asthma
8 hay fever
9 the countryside

Activities for Part 3

1 Hats page 100

1A 2D 3B 4B 5D 6B

2 Saving Australia page 101

1C 2D 3D 4B 5B 6A 7B 8D 9A

3 Two-star chef page 102

A Multiple choice questions
1B 2C 3D 4C 5B 6A 7D 8B 9D
B Identify the comments the speakers make
1N 2A 3A 4M 5A 6M 7N 8N 9A
10M 11M 12A 13M

4 Touring holiday page 103

A Multiple choice questions
1A 2C 3D 4C 5D 6C 7A 8B
B Identify the comments the speakers make
1N 2J 3N 4G 5N 6J 7N 8J 9N
10G 11G 12G 13N 14J 15O

Activities for Part 4

1 Relationships page 104

Task one 1F 2E 3G 4C 5D
Task two 6F 7B 8A 9G 10E

2 Class distinction page 105

A Multiple matching
Task one 1J 2C 3E 4A 5G
Task two 6I 7F 8E 9H 10A
B Multiple choice
1B 2A 3C 4B 5B 6B 7C 8B 9A
10B

3 Food page 106

Task one 1C 2F 3H 4G 5D
Task two 6C 7A 8H 9B 10E

4 Coping with the unexpected page 107

Task one 1B 2D 3A 4C 5E
Task two 6C 7G 8B 9A 10H